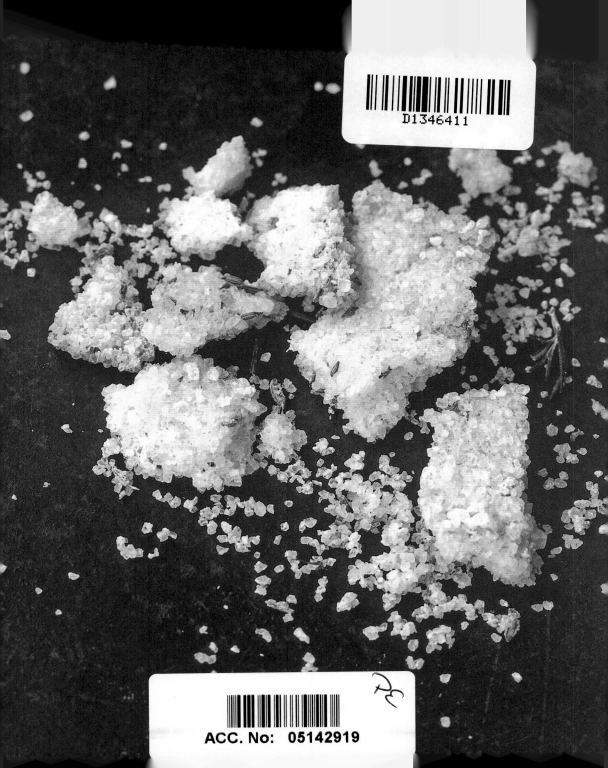

SALT & PEPPER

SALT & PEPPER

COOKING WITH THE WORLD'S MOST POPULAR SEASONINGS

VALERIE AIKMAN-SMITH

RYLAND PETERS & SMALL

LONDON • NEW YORK

Senior Designer Toni Kay
Head of Production Patricia Harrington
Art Director Leslie Harrington
Editorial Director Julia Charles
Publisher Cindy Richards
Food Stylist Valerie Aikman-Smith
Indexer Hilary Bird

First published in 2019 by
Ryland Peters & Small
20–21 Jockey's Fields
London WC1R 4BW
and
341 E 116th St
New York NY 10029

www.rylandpeters.com

10 9 8 7 6 5 4 3 2 1

Text copyright © Valerie Aikman-Smith
2009, 2016, 2019

Design and photographs © Ryland
Peters & Small 2009, 2016, 2019

Recipes in this book have been
previously published by Ryland
Peters & Small.

ISBN: 978-1-78879-122-9

Printed in China

A CIP record for this book is available from
the British Library. US Library of Congress
Cataloging-in-Publication Data has been
applied for.

Notes:
• Both British (Metric) and American
(Imperial plus US cups) measurements
are included in these recipes for your
convenience, however it is important to
work with one set of measurements and not
alternate between the two within a recipe.
• All spoon measurements are level
unless otherwise specified.
• All eggs are medium (UK) or large (US),
unless specified as large, in which case
US extra-large should be used.
• Ovens should be preheated to the
specified temperatures. If you are using
a fan-assisted oven, adjust temperatures
according to the manufacturer's instructions.
• When a recipe calls for the grated zest of
citrus fruit, buy unwaxed fruit.

CONTENTS

INTRODUCING SALT

Salt, heavenly salt—every cook's pantry is stocked with it, from everyday cooking salt to the pink rock salt of the Himalayas or the aromatic fleur de sel harvested in Guérande, France. There are flavored salts, spiced salts, smoked salts, and salts of the most beautiful hues.

We use this magical ingredient in everything; whether it's for sprinkling over an omelet or decorating the rim of a margarita glass.

We season, preserve, bake, cure, brine, pickle, and make rubs with this wonderful ingredient. Harvested from land and sea, it comes in a multitude of shapes, textures, colors, and tastes. Just a sprinkle of this divine substance can make a dish sing.

Cooks delight in their collections of salts from all over the world. They love to discuss the effects of salt and how they use it to add a freshness and piquancy to food. Some people with a strong devotion to salt even go so far as to carry around a small salt shaker/cellar with them.

Salt has been a prized possession since the beginning of civilization. It was once used as a form of currency and wars have been won and lost over it. Nations have been taxed on their salt. In China, salt tax revenues were used to build the Great Wall. The Greeks and the Mayans worshipped their gods with salt offerings. Roman soldiers were given an allowance of salt known as "salarium," from which the word "salary" comes. There are salt routes all over the world that were used to transport salt from continent to continent. In Italy one of the oldest roads is called Via Salaria, meaning "salt route," and Venice has a long history of making herbed salts. At one time salt was so precious it was traded ounce for ounce with gold.

So where does the salt that we buy come from? It is mined deep in the earth and harvested from salt lakes or salt pans. Salt lakes are naturally occurring inland bodies of water, which are remnants of ancient seas. Salt pans are man-made basins, situated next to the sea, which are flooded with salt waters. These in turn evaporate in the sun and the salt that is left behind is harvested. Wherever it comes from in the world we are always surprised and delighted to have it around.

Remember if you spill salt, throw a pinch of it over your shoulder for good luck.

SALT DIRECTORY

1 Rock salt
This is mined from salt deposits deep in the earth and is sometimes colored with minerals. It has a large grain, which makes it ideal for use when cooking with a salt crust, but otherwise it is usually put in a salt grinder for easier use.

2 Murray River salt flakes
These delicate pink salt flakes come from the Murray River region in Australia. They are harvested from pure underground saline waters rich in minerals, giving them their wonderful taste and pink color. Good for cooking and as a pretty garnish.

3 Himalayan pink rock salt
This salt is hand-mined in Nepal from ancient salt deposits and is believed to be the purest salt on earth. The iron content gives it its distinct pink color. Fun to have in a block and grate over food.

4 Green tea salt
This salt is made by mixing matcha, a Japanese green tea powder, with sea salt and grinding it to a fine powder using a mortar and pestle. It adds a gentle taste when sprinkled on salads and is high in amino acids.

5 Smoked salts
Smoked salts are man-made by smoking the salts with flavored wood chips. They come in versions such as mesquite or hickory and add a deep flavor to dishes.

6 Hawaiian black lava sea salt
Harvested sea salt is mixed with crushed black lava and black charcoal, which give it its dark color. It should be sprinkled on food only at the last minute. Do not immerse it in liquid as it will lose its color in the process.

7 Sea salt flakes
These are large delicate salt crystals made from the evaporation by the sun on the sea or salt lakes. Rich in minerals, they come in an array of colors depending on their geographical origin.

8 Hawaiian red alaea sea salt
This salt hails from the island of Kauai. "Alaea" is the name given to the natural mineral found in the run-off from the volcano, which occurs in the rainy season. It is a red clay which colors the salt pans a deep shade of burnt red. This salt is used mostly for garnishing dishes.

9 Sel gris
Sel gris (gray/grey salt) is also known as Celtic sea salt. Hand-harvested from the bottom of the salt flats in Guérande, France, it gets its color from the clay in the beds.

10 Jurassic salt
Jurassic salt gets its name from the era 150 million years ago when Utah was mostly under water. When the water dried up, it left behind this mineral-intense salt with a pinkish hue. This salt has a delicate flavor and is perfect for most types of cooking, especially baking.

11 Fleur de sel
A hand-harvested sea salt from the Guérande and Camargue regions in France. The crystallized salt is skimmed from the surface of the salt pans, flooded with the waters of the Mediterranean. It has a mild flavor.

Flavored salts
These are made with fruits, spices, fresh and dried herbs, pounded together with salt using a mortar and pestle. If you use fresh herbs or fruits, crush then spread them out on a baking sheet and place in a low temperature oven for 30 minutes before mixing with salt.

BRINES

Remember, once you have brined foods you must throw away the brine mixture; it cannot be re-used for anything else.

BEER BRINE

Brining ribs and chops really keeps them moist when they hit that fiery grill of a barbecue. You can leave meats in the brine for 2–3 days; the longer the better.

4 cups/1 litre boiling water
1 bottle Guinness or dark beer
1/4 cup/60 g coarse rock salt
3 tablespoons dark brown sugar
3 tablespoons molasses
1 tablespoon dried oregano

MAKES 6 CUPS/1.5 LITRES

Put all the ingredients in a large bowl, stir until dissolved, and set aside. When the brine has cooled completely, it is ready to use.

CHILE/CHILLI BRINE

This chile brine is excellent for shrimp/prawns in their shells. Only brine seafood for 20 minutes; after that the meat will begin to break up.

1/4 cup/60 g sea salt
2 tablespoons dark brown sugar
6 dried red chiles/chillies
1 tablespoon coriander seeds
4 kaffir lime leaves

MAKES 6 1/2 CUPS/1.75 LITRES

Put all of the ingredients in a saucepan with 6 cups/1.5 litres water and bring to a boil. Let simmer for 5 minutes. Set aside. When the brine has cooled completely, it is ready to use.

SWEET TEA BRINE

Infusing chicken in this sweet tea brine gives the final dish a special taste. Fruity and light, it is the perfect brine for fried chicken.

4 tablespoons black tea leaves
6 cups/1.5 litres boiling water
1/4 cup/60 g coarse rock salt
3 tablespoons dark brown sugar
1/4 cup/60 ml honey

MAKES 6 1/2 CUPS/1.75 LITRES

Put the black tea leaves in a measuring pitcher/jug and pour over the boiling water. Add the salt, sugar, and honey and stir until dissolved. Set aside until completely cool before using.

PICKLED LIMES

Pickled limes are a great way to jazz up recipes. They're quick and easy to make and are ready in 1 month.

1 cup/225 g sea salt
12 limes, quartered
5 kaffir lime leaves
1 tablespoon pink peppercorns
freshly squeezed juice of 6 limes

a sterilized 1-quart/litre capacity jar*

MAKES 1 QUART/LITRE

Put 1 tablespoon salt in the jar and layer with 4 lime quarters. Sprinkle with 2 tablespoons salt, then put 2 kaffir lime leaves and a few peppercorns on top. Continue to layer in this way, packing the limes down firmly as you go, until the jar is full. You may need to push the limes down.

Finish with a layer of salt and pour the lime juice over, to cover the limes. Seal the jar and store in a cool, dark place for 1 month before using. Only serve the skins of the limes; cut away and discard the pith and flesh.

*To sterilize, wash the jar in hot soapy water and rinse. Put the jar in a preheated oven at 180°C (350°F) Gas 4 for 10 minutes.

From left: Sweet Tea Brine, Chile/Chilli Brine, Pickled Limes, and Beer Brine.

INTRODUCING PEPPER

The mighty little peppercorn—once known as the "king of spices"—is a mainstay in any cook's kitchen.

Each time I pick up my peppermill, I am immediately transported to the faraway exotic lands this tiny, robust, jewel-like spice comes from, and reminded of its importance throughout history. Alongside salt and other spices, historically pepper played a powerful role in shaping trade routes around the world and creating wealth for the spice merchants. It's also a prominent feature in Indian Ayurvedic medicine and is used to help relieve many conditions, including colds and coughs—even Greek physician Hippocrates mixed pepper with other spices to treat fevers and the Ancient Romans believed it an antidote to poison.

Small and colorful, peppercorns are packed with an arsenal of flavors, which range from fiery and spicy to earthy, and even include bright citrus tones. The berries grow in clusters on a tropical vine (*Piper nigrum*) and are picked and dried in the sun. Originating in India, pepper is now cultivated on a commercial scale in Vietnam, Brazil, Indonesia, China, and Malaysia.

There is a wide variety of pepper to choose from, depending on whether you are baking, seasoning marinades and rubs, or flavoring preserves. Use brightly colored peppercorns to cure and pickle. Stir freshly ground white pepper into a creamy, silky Béchamel sauce and drizzle over pan-roasted fish. Add a little heat to curries and stir fries by using crushed Szechuan peppercorns. Season thick-cut steaks with robust Tellicherry pepper and make classic French sauces with briny green peppercorns. Mix with fresh spices and place in your peppermill to grind as a finishing touch over pastas, soups, and salads. If you are lucky, you may to be able to locate fresh peppercorns and they can be stirred into slow-cooked stews and curries.

Buy peppercorns from the freshest source and in small quantities, as they tend to lose their punch after about six months. Specialist spice shops or online stores are the best place, as in supermarkets they may lose their flavor by sitting on the shelves for too long. Look out for Fairtrade labels and buy organic wherever possible. Make sure the peppercorns have a good color and a strong aroma. Buy them whole so that you can crack or grind them in a peppermill or pestle and mortar. Store in airtight containers and place in a cool, dark cupboard before filling up your peppermill.

PEPPER DIRECTORY

1 Rainbow peppercorns
A mix of green, red, white, and black peppercorns, which gives a lively look to any food when freshly ground.

2 Green peppercorns
Harvested in the Mysore region in southern India, these come from the same plant as black peppercorns and are picked unripe. They are an earthy green color and have a wonderful fresh, bright flavor.

3 Sansho peppercorns
Harvested in Kochi, Japan and similar to Szechuan peppercorns with their heat and tingly, numbing effect. These are the unripe fruit from the ash tree and are wonderfully fiery, with a divine citrus flavor.

4 & 5 Brined peppercorns
Green peppercorns brined in salt water have a more intense taste than dried peppercorns. They give dishes a powerful, earthy heat that works well in sauces and pâtés. They are used extensively in Asian cooking in soups.

6 Tellicherry peppercorns
Left to mature for longer on the vine, these have a deep, dark, bold flavor and are a little larger than regular peppercorns. Hailing from the Malabar coast of south-west India, they are picked when red, then left to dry and turn black in the sun.

7 Pink peppercorns
These gorgeous, bright pink, jewel-like peppercorns originally came from the French island of Réunion in the Indian Ocean. Today they are mostly grown in Brazil. Although not a true peppercorn, they have similar traits with a sweet taste and a little heat.

8 Lampong black peppercorns
Cultivated in Indonesia, these peppercorns are not allowed to stay on the vine for long and are picked as soon as they ripen, which yields a sweet, woody, and hot flavor. They work well with all types of food, but especially with Asian cuisine.

9 Smoked peppercorns
These black peppercorns have been slowly smoked in flavors such as hickory, mesquite, and bourbon. There are many artisanal smoking recipes to choose from. The smoky, dark, robust flavors work really well in rubs, marinades, and sauces.

10 Szechuan peppercorns
These are not truly peppercorns. They are native to Szechuan province in China and are the outer shell of the fruit from an aromatic shrub in the rue family. They have a jewel-like tone of dark red and pale green and have a wonderful fiery numbing taste that then gives way to sweetness.

11 White peppercorns
These come from Sarawak in Borneo where they are grown on small farms. Picked black and ripe, they are then soaked in water to soften and remove the shell. They have a musky aroma and are hotter than most black peppercorns. They are good for seasoning white sauces and cheese dishes.

12 Long pepper
These grow on a luscious green, shiny, flowering vine with small black pepper spikes. Harvested in India and Indonesia, long pepper is known for its healing remedies. It has a fruity aroma and a good heat that lingers.

13 Malabar peppercorns
Harvested in the state of Kerala on India's Malabar coast, they are picked and dried in the sun where they turn black. They have a unique sharp heat with a robust, sweet earthiness.

PEPPERMILL MIXES

Use these mixes to flavor stews, pasta dishes, and stir fries, to infuse oils and pickles, or mix into oil to make a wet rub or marinade.

Each mix uses the same method. Mix all the ingredients together and store in a glass jar with a tight fitting lid. To use, spoon the mix into a peppermill.

MOROCCAN ROSE PETAL

$1^1/_2$ heaped teaspoons Tellicherry
  peppercorns
$1^1/_2$ teaspoons caraway seeds
$1/_2$ teaspoon ground cardamom
$1^1/_2$ teaspoons dried hot
  red pepper/chilli flakes
2 long peppercorns (*Piper longum*)
$1/_2$ cinnamon stick, crushed
$1/_2$ cup/60 g edible dried organic
  rose petals
1 teaspoon pink peppercorns

DRIED HIBISCUS

$1/_3$ cup/45 g edible dried organic
  hibiscus flowers, crushed
1 tablespoon pink peppercorns
2 long peppercorns (*Piper longum*)

CITRUS PEPPER

3 tablespoons white peppercorns
1 tablespoon dried lemon peel
1 tablespoon dried orange peel

CHINESE FIVE-SPICE PEPPER

2 tablespoons Szechuan peppercorns
1 cinnamon stick, crushed
2 teaspoons allspice berries,
  crushed
1 teaspoon whole cloves
1 teaspoon ground ginger
1 teaspoon fennel seeds

HACHIMI TOGARASHI

2 teaspoons Sansho peppercorns
1 sheet of nori seaweed, crumbled
  (about 2 tablespoons)
2 teaspoons black sesame seeds
2 teaspoons dried orange peel
1 teaspoon dried hot red pepper/chilli
  flakes
1 teaspoon chilli powder
$1/_2$ teaspoon ground ginger
$1/_2$ teaspoon garlic powder

SMOKED PEPPER

2 tablespoons smoked black
  peppercorns
1 tablespoon dried hot
  red pepper/chilli flakes
1 teaspoon coarse garlic powder
1 teaspoon fenugreek seeds
2 teaspoons smoked paprika
1 dried bay leaf, crumbled

BERBERE PEPPER

2 tablespoons Malabar peppercorns
1 tablespoon ground hot paprika
1 teaspoon ground paprika
1 teaspoon ground cardamom
1 teaspoon ground ginger
1 cinnamon stick, crushed
1 teaspoon allspice berries
1 teaspoon coarse garlic powder
$1/_2$ teaspoon fenugreek seeds

Clockwise from top left: *Hachimi Togarashi, Chinese Five-spice Pepper, Moroccan Rose Petal, Dried Hibiscus, Smoked Pepper, Berbere Pepper, Citrus Pepper.*

PRESERVES, PICKLES & DRESSINGS

PEPPERED PEACH CHUTNEY

In summer when peaches are on sale in the markets, make a batch of this delicious chutney. The punch comes from the black Kerala peppercorns that impart a wonderfully bold flavor.

12 firm ripe peaches, halved and pitted/stoned
4 yellow onions, roughly chopped
5 garlic cloves, finely chopped
2 teaspoons each of ground cumin, ground coriander, chilli powder, whole Kerala peppercorns, and curry powder
1 teaspoon mustard seeds
2 cinnamon sticks
3 bay leaves
1½ cups/355 ml apple cider vinegar
2¼ cups/450 g demerara or turbinado sugar

MAKES ABOUT 5 CUPS/1.15 LITRES

Preheat the oven to 200°C (400°F) Gas 6.

Cut the peaches into 2-inch/5-cm pieces and put in a ceramic baking dish. Add the remaining ingredients apart from the sugar, and toss to combine. Bake in the preheated oven for 40 minutes, stirring halfway through. Add the sugar and stir. Return to the oven for another 55 minutes. Check every 15 minutes and stir to prevent burning.

Remove from the oven and allow it to sit for 5 minutes, then spoon into sterilized jars, leaving ¼-inch/ 5-mm space at the top. Screw on the lids. Cool, then store in the fridge for 7–10 days before eating. Once open, store in the fridge for up to 3 months.

TOMATO & SMOKED PEPPER JAM

Dollop this spicy, smoky condiment on top of a burger or serve alongside anything that comes off a fiery hot barbecue in the heat of the summer. It also makes a perfect partner to a cheeseboard for a casual get-together.

4 lbs./1.8 kg tomatoes
2 tablespoons extra virgin olive oil
1 teaspoon sea salt
2 cups/400 g dark brown sugar
1 tablespoon harissa
1 tablespoon cracked smoked black peppercorns
1 cinnamon stick
2 tablespoons freshly squeezed lemon juice

MAKES ABOUT 3 CUPS/700 ML

Preheat the oven to 200°C (400°F) Gas 6.

Spread the tomatoes evenly on a baking sheet. Pour over the olive oil and sprinkle with the salt. Roast in the preheated oven for 40 minutes until the skins have burst and are slightly charred.

Put in a food processor and pulse until coarsely chopped, then tip into a medium-sized pan and add the sugar, harissa, peppercorns, and cinnamon stick. Bring to a boil over a medium-high heat, stirring continuously. Reduce the heat to a simmer and cook for 40 minutes, stirring occasionally until the mixture becomes dark and thickens. Add the lemon juice and cook for a further 5 minutes.

Pour the jam into sterilized jars and screw the lids on. When cool, store in the fridge for up to 1 month.

PEPPER PICKLES

Pickles are wonderfully fresh and crunchy. Each recipe makes about 2 cups/500 g. To seal, screw the lid on the jars while still warm, turn upside down to cool completely, then put in the fridge for at least 1 week before eating or storing in the cupboard. Once opened, consume within 6 months.

BASIC PICKLE MIX

2 cups/475 ml white wine vinegar
1/2 cup/100 g sugar
1 teaspoon coarse sea salt
1 bay leaf

WATERMELON RIND

5 lbs./2.25 kg mini watermelon
3 tablespoons coarse sea salt
2 cups/475 ml white wine vinegar
1 cup/200 g white sugar
1 tablespoon rainbow peppercorns
2 teaspoons Piment d'Espelette
    or hot red pepper/dried chilli flakes

Cut the watermelon into wedges and scoop the flesh out, leaving 1/2 inch/1 cm of flesh attached to the rind, then cut into small cubes.

Pour 6 cups/1.4 litres water into a saucepan, add the salt, and bring to a boil. Add the watermelon rind and boil for 5 minutes, then drain and pour into a large jar.

In a pan bring the vinegar to a boil with the sugar,

peppercorns, and Piment d'Espelette or hot red pepper/ dried chilli flakes, stirring to dissolve the sugar. Cook for 5 minutes, then pour over the fruit and seal as above.

PEPPERY CUCUMBERS

6 Persian cucumbers, thinly sliced
1 quantity of Basic Pickle Mix
1 1/2 teaspoons Szechuan peppercorns

Layer the cucumbers in a sterilized jar. Bring the Basic Pickle Mix and the peppercorns to a boil, stirring to dissolve the sugar. Cook for 3 minutes, then pour into the jar and seal as above.

SPICY KUMQUATS

24 kumquats, halved
3 jalapeños, thinly sliced
1 cinnamon stick
2 star anise
2 teaspoons Malabar peppercorns
1 quantity of Basic Pickle Mix

Layer all the ingredients except for the Basic Pickle Mix in a sterilized jar. Bring the Basic Pickle Mix to a boil, stirring to dissolve the sugar, and cook for 3 minutes, then pour into the jar and seal as above.

JAPANESE RADISHES

4 watermelon (or 6 regular) radishes
12 shishito (or Padrón) peppers, sliced
3 jalapeños, thinly sliced
1 1/2 teaspoons Sansho pepper
1 quantity of Basic Pickle Mix
1/4 cup/60 ml sake (rice wine)

Layer all the ingredients except for the Basic Pickle Mix and sake in a sterilized jar. Bring the Basic Pickle Mix and sake to a boil, stirring to dissolve the sugar. Cook for 3 minutes, then pour into the jar and seal as above.

Clockwise from top left: *Peppery Cucumbers, Watermelon Rind, Carrots & Raisins (p.81), Chai Apples (p.135), Spicy Kumquats, Curried Cauliflower (p.51), Japanese Radishes.*

MUSTARDS

Mustards are quick and easy to make. Use the same method for each of the mustards.

GREEN PEPPERCORN

1/2 cup/75 g yellow
  mustard seeds
3/4 cup/175 ml cider vinegar
2 tablespoons cracked
  green peppercorns
2 tablespoons dark
  brown sugar
1 teaspoon freshly
  squeezed lemon juice
1 teaspoon sea salt

SMOKED PEPPER

1/2 cup/75 g yellow
  mustard seeds
3/4 cup/175 ml cider vinegar
1 tablespoon cracked
  smoked black peppercorns
1 tablespoon harissa
1/2 teaspoon ancho
  chili/chilli powder

2 tablespoons dark
  brown sugar
1 teaspoon freshly squeezed
  lemon juice
1 teaspoon sea salt

PORT &
BLACK PEPPER

1/2 cup/75 g cup yellow
  mustard seeds
1/2 cup/120 ml red
  wine vinegar
1/4 cup/60 ml port
2 tablespoons cracked
  Tellicherry black
  peppercorns
2 tablespoons dark
  brown sugar
1 teaspoon sea salt

**EACH MAKES ABOUT
1 CUP/250 G**

Dry-roast the mustard seeds in a hot pan for 2 minutes, then tip into a bowl and add the vinegar. Leave to soak overnight. Pour the mustard seeds and all the remaining ingredients into a blender. Process, adding a little more vinegar if the mixture is too stiff. Pour into sterilized jars, screw the lids on and refrigerate for up to 2 months.

INFUSED OILS

Choose different kinds of oils, herbs, spices, nuts, and fruits to make small batches of infused oils using the same method for each recipe.

SZECHUAN
CHILE/CHILLI

1 cup/235 ml sunflower oil
2 tablespoons Szechuan
  peppercorns

PEPPER MADRAS

1 cup/235 ml sunflower oil
1 1/2 tablespoons long
  peppercorns
2 teaspoons Madras
  curry powder

PEPPER GINGER

1 cup/235 ml sunflower oil
1/3 cup/50 g crystallized
  ginger
1 tablespoon Malabar
  peppercorns

RAINBOW ROSEMARY

1 cup/235 ml olive oil
2 tablespoons rainbow
  peppercorns
2 sprigs of rosemary

**EACH MAKES ABOUT
1 CUP/250 ML**

Pour the oil into a small saucepan and bring to a simmer. Turn off the heat and add the remaining ingredients. Cool overnight. Next day, strain through a coffee filter into a sterilized glass jar with a lid (you can also leave it unstrained if you prefer). Store in the fridge for up to 1 month.

Clockwise from top left: Szechuan Chili/Chilli Oil, Rainbow Rosemary Oil, Pepper Madras Oil, Port & Black Pepper Mustard, Smoked Pepper Mustard, Green Peppercorn Mustard, Pepper Ginger Oil.

BUTTERS

To make these butters, except the Salty Peanut Butter, blend the ingredients in a food processor until smooth. For ease of serving, put the butter mixture on a piece of plastic wrap/clingfilm. Roll into a sausage shape. Twist the ends, refrigerate, and when firm slice the butter into discs to use. Each recipe makes about 1/2 cup/120 g unless otherwise indicated.

LEMON CAPER BUTTER

This simple butter goes perfectly with pan-fried fish.

1 stick/115 g unsalted butter
finely grated zest and freshly
   squeezed juice of 1 small lemon
1 tablespoon salted capers
   (do not rinse off the salt)

GREEN PEPPER BUTTER

This can be used to make a quick Steak au Poivre; simply melt a dollop on a grilled steak.

1 stick/115 g unsalted butter
2 tablespoons brined green peppercorns
sel gris and cracked black pepper, to taste

INDIAN BUTTER

This butter is excellent spread on naan bread and warmed under the broiler/grill, or mix a tablespoon through basmati rice just before serving.

1 teaspoon each coriander seeds
   and cumin seeds, dry-roasted
   in a small pan until light brown
1 stick/115 g unsalted butter

1 garlic clove, chopped
1 teaspoon smoked paprika
1 teaspoon chili/chilli powder
1 teaspoon curry powder
1 teaspoon sea salt
cracked black pepper, to taste

TUNA BUTTER

This is a variation of tonnato sauce. It's perfect to finish off a piece of grilled fish or chicken.

1 stick/115 g unsalted butter
2 oz./60 g canned tuna, drained
finely grated zest and freshly
   squeezed juice of 1 small lemon
1 teaspoon Dijon mustard
1 tablespoon salted capers
cracked black pepper, to taste

MAKES 3/4 CUP/180 G

ANCHOVY BUTTER

The sharpness of cornichons brings out the saltiness of the anchovies. Perfect for spreading on fresh wholemeal bread.

1 stick/115 g unsalted butter
4 salted anchovy fillets
1 oz./30 g cornichons, chopped
finely grated zest and juice of
   1 small lemon
cracked black pepper, to taste

SALTY PEANUT BUTTER

Homemade peanut butter is so different from store-bought. If you can't find old-fashioned blistered peanuts, regular salted peanuts also work well.

1 1/2 cups/190 g salted blistered peanuts
1/4 cup/60 ml peanut oil

MAKES 1 CUP/250 G

Put the peanuts in a food processor. With the motor running, pour in the peanut oil in a steady stream. Process until incorporated.

Clockwise from top: Lemon Caper Butter, Tuna Butter, Indian Butter, Salty Peanut Butter, Green Pepper Butter, Anchovy Butter.

DIPS & PASTES

These are easy to make, often from cupboard ingredients. Each of the dip recipes makes 2–3 servings and the Harissa 2 cups/220 g.

ANCHOÏADE

Serve this Provençal dip spread onto toasted slices of baguette.

2 oz./55 g anchovy fillets in oil
3 garlic cloves, finely chopped
1/2 teaspoon herbes de Provence
grated zest and juice of 1/2 lemon
1 oz./30 g blanched almonds
2 tablespoons dried Italian parsley
2 tablespoons olive oil
1/2 teaspoon fleur de sel
cracked black pepper, to taste

Put all the ingredients except the pepper in a food processor and blend to a thick paste. Season with pepper.

MUHAMMARA

A refreshing Middle Eastern dip to enjoy with warm flatbreads.

1 cup/115 g walnuts halves
1/2 cup/115 g fresh brown breadcrumbs
1 hot red chile/chilli, chopped
1 garlic clove, roughly chopped
3 tablespoons pomegranate molasses
1/2 teaspoon each ground cumin, coriander, and smoked paprika
3/4 cup/90 g fresh pomegranate seeds
1/2 cup/125 ml walnut oil, plus to drizzle

salt, to taste
a handful of mint leaves, to serve

Toast the walnuts in a small pan for 2–3 minutes. Let cool, then put in a food processor with the other ingredients, reserving one third of the pomegranate seeds. Process until slightly chunky. Season with sea salt. Garnish with the remaining seeds, torn mint leaves, and a drizzle of walnut oil.

DUKKAH

Enjoy this Egyptian treat by dipping bread in olive oil and then into the dukkah.

1/4 cup/40 g each of hazelnuts, fennel seeds, cumin seeds, and coriander seeds
3 oz./80 g sesame seeds
1 teaspoon sel gris
1/2 teaspoon cracked black pepper

Toast the hazelnuts and each of the spices separately in a small pan. Let cool slightly, then put in a food processor and pulse a few times.

BAGNA CAUDA

Dip grilled vegetables into this sauce.

4 garlic cloves, roughly chopped
1/2 cup/120 g anchovy fillets in oil
grated zest of 1 lemon and juice of 1/2 lemon
1/4 cup/60 ml olive oil
black pepper and sea salt, to taste

In a food processor, mix the garlic and anchovies. Transfer to a small pan, add the lemon zest and juice and warm over low heat. Gradually add the oil until just warmed through. Season with pepper and salt.

HARISSA

Use this spicy North African chili/chilli paste as a flavoring or rub.

1 teaspoon each cumin and coriander seeds
3 small roasted red (bell) peppers
3 hot red chiles/chillies, roughly chopped
1 garlic clove, roughly chopped
1/2 teaspoon Jurassic salt
1/4 cup/60 ml olive oil

Toast the cumin and coriander seeds in a small pan. Peel the roasted peppers. Put everything in a food processor and process until smooth. Store in a screwtop glass jar.

Clockwise from top right: Pink Salt Herbes de Provence Rub (p.90), Anchoïade, Muhammara, Harissa, Bagna Cauda, Dukkah.

SMALL BITES & SNACKS

HARICOTS VERTS TEMPURA

Tempura green beans dusted with Hachimi Togarashi is a match made in heaven.

1½ cups/200 g rice flour
½ teaspoon ground Hachimi Togarashi peppermill mix (p.16), plus extra for dusting
½ teaspoon sea salt
1 egg

1¼ cups/350 ml club soda/ soda water
vegetable oil, for frying
1 lb./450 g haricots verts, trimmed

SERVES 4

Put all the ingredients except the oil and haricots verts in a blender and process for about 30 seconds until mixed, then pour into a shallow bowl.

Pour enough oil to come halfway up a wide medium-sized saucepan, then set over a medium–high heat until the oil starts to simmer.

Working in batches, dip the beans in the batter and deep fry for 3–4 minutes until golden and cooked. Transfer to a wire rack to drain, dust with Hachimi Togarashi, and serve.

ROASTED CHICKPEAS

Spicy, crunchy, and extremely moreish!

1 tablespoon harissa paste
1 tablespoon extra virgin olive oil
1 teaspoon cracked smoked peppercorns
1 teaspoon ground coriander
1 teaspoon ground cumin

1 teaspoon sea salt
2 x 14-oz./400-g cans of chickpeas, drained and rinsed

SERVES 8–10

Preheat the oven to 200°C (400°F) Gas 6.

In a bowl whisk together the harissa, oil, pepper, coriander, cumin, and salt until combined. Add the chickpeas and toss to coat.

Spread the chickpeas out in an even layer on a baking sheet and roast in the preheated oven for 30 minutes. Shake the pan halfway through cooking. Remove from the oven and cool before serving. Store in an airtight container for up to 1 week.

STREET HAWKER TEA EGGS

Sold as street food in China, these eggs make a fun addition to a Chinese feast.

6 eggs, hard-boiled/ hard-cooked
1 black tea bag
4 star anise
1 teaspoon five-spice powder
2 teaspoons cracked Szechuan pepper

1 cinnamon stick
½ cup/120 ml soy sauce
sea salt and ground Chinese Five-spice peppermill mix (p.16), to serve

MAKES 6

Gently roll the eggs on a work surface to crack the eggshells all over.

Put the remaining ingredients except those to serve into a pan and pour over 2 cups/475 ml water. Bring to a boil over a high heat, then reduce to a simmer and cook for 5 minutes.

Remove from the heat and add the eggs to the saucepan. Allow the liquid to cool, then refrigerate overnight.

Remove the eggs from the liquid and peel. Cut in half and sprinkle with salt and some Chinese Five-spice peppermill mix.

HOMEMADE RICOTTA CHEESE IN A PEPPER CRUST

There's a taste of the souk in this pepper crust with the glorious delicate perfume of rose petals.

4 cups/950 ml whole milk
1/2 cup/120 ml heavy/double cream
1 teaspoon coarse sea salt
1 1/2 tablespoons organic distilled white wine vinegar
2 tablespoons ground Moroccan Rose Petal peppermill mix (p.16)

MAKES ABOUT 2 CUPS/450 G

Put the milk, cream, and salt in a large pan and bring to a boil. Remove from the heat and add the vinegar. Stir, then cover and set aside to cool.

Line a strainer/sieve with muslin/cheesecloth and place over a large bowl. Strain into a bowl. Cover and refrigerate overnight.

Roll the cheese up tightly in a piece of plastic wrap/clingfilm. Unwrap and roll in the pepper mix to serve.

VINE-ROASTED GRAPES

Inspired by Californian wine country, these grapes are a wonderful addition to a cheeseboard or salad.

1 lb./450 g seedless red grapes on the vine
1 tablespoon extra virgin olive oil
2 teaspoons fennel pollen or ground fennel
1 teaspoon cracked Tellicherry black peppercorns
1 teaspoon coarse sea salt
6 sprigs of fresh thyme

MAKES 1 LB./450 G

Preheat the oven to 190°C (375°F) Gas 5.

Put the grapes in a large ovenproof dish. Drizzle with the oil, then sprinkle with the fennel, pepper, and salt. Gently turn the grapes to coat with mixture. Place the sprigs of thyme on and around the grapes. Roast in the preheated oven for 45 minutes, turning halfway through.

The roasted grapes are best served at room temperature.

PEPPER-INFUSED HONEY

Serve this briny, peppery honey drizzled over cheese or grilled meats or whisked into vinaigrette. Try stirring it into a cocktail for an unusual twist.

2 strings of brined green peppercorns (if you can't buy strings of peppercorns, use 2 tablespoons instead)
2 cups/560 g organic wildflower honey

MAKES 2 CUPS/560 G

Place the peppercorns in a sterilized jar with a tightly fitting lid. Pour in the honey and screw on the lid. Leave to infuse for 1 week before using. The longer you leave the honey, the more intense the taste.

VINE-WRAPPED FETA PARCELS

A taste of Greece in a pan, salty feta sprinkled with citrus pepper and wrapped up in a briny vine leaf makes a wonderful mezze dish for sharing.

1 lb./450 g feta cheese
24 brined vine leaves
2 tablespoons ground Citrus Pepper peppermill mix
   (p.16)
peel of 1 lemon, cut into strips
olive oil, to cover

MAKES 24

Cut the feta into 24 cubes. Lay the vine leaves out on a worksurface and place a piece of feta at the stem end of each leaf. Sprinkle with the peppermill mix.

Fold the two sides of the leaf over the feta, then roll the leaf up like a cigar. Repeat to make 24 parcels. Place the feta parcels in a glass dish. Sprinkle with the lemon peel and pour olive oil over to cover.

Cover and refrigerate for at least 1 week before serving. The parcels will keep for up to 1 month in the fridge.

PEPPERED PAN-ROASTED OLIVES

Jeweled bright green Italian Castelvetrano olives are perfect for pan frying. Mixed with citrus and salty capers, they offer a taste of the Italian countryside.

2 tablespoons olive oil
8 oz./225 g unpitted Castelvetrano olives
2 slices of dried tangerine or orange
1/2 teaspoon crushed Smoked Pepper peppermill mix
   (p.16)
2 teaspoons salted capers

SERVES 4–6

Heat the oil in a skillet/frying pan over a medium heat. Add the olives, dried tangerine slices, peppermill mix, and salted capers and fry for 3–4 minutes.

Tip into a bowl and serve immediately.

SPICY POPCORN
WITH CHIPOTLE SALT

You can't watch a movie without snacks. My popcorn has a fabulous pink tint and chile/chilli kick.

4 tablespoons Murray River Australian pink salt flakes
2 tablespoons chipotle powder, or to taste
2 bags unsalted microwave popcorn

SERVES 4

In a small bowl, mix together the salt and chipotle powder. Cook the popcorn according to the instructions on the packet.

When it has popped, put in a large bowl. Sprinkle with the chipotle salt while still warm and toss to coat.

GOLD POTATO CHIPS
WITH TRUFFLE SALT

Potatoes, truffles, and salt are a match made in heaven. Use a mandoline to slice the potatoes wafer thin.

1 lb./500 g Yukon Gold or any other good all-purpose potatoes (about 6 small), unpeeled
vegetable oil, for deep-frying
truffle salt, to sprinkle

an electric deep-fat fryer
a deep-frying thermometer

SERVES 4–6

Wash and dry the potatoes, slice thinly, and set aside.

Heat the oil in the deep-fat fryer or a heavy-bottomed pan until it reaches 180°C (350°F). To test if it is hot enough, drop a cube of bread in the oil and it should turn golden brown in about 20 seconds.

Fry the potato slices in batches and drain on paper towels.

Put the drained potato crisps in a bowl, sprinkle with truffle salt, toss, and serve.

CANDIED SALTED ALMONDS

2 cups/270 g raw almonds, skin on
1/2 cup/60 g dark brown sugar
1/4 cup/60 g maple syrup
1 teaspoon chipotle powder
1 tablespoon sel gris, coarsely ground

MAKES 2 CUPS/300 G

Preheat the oven to 190°C (375°F) Gas 5.

Mix all the ingredients except for the sel gris together in a bowl until the almonds are well coated. Spread the almonds on a non-stick baking sheet and bake in the preheated oven for 5–8 minutes. The sugars will bubble and turn a few shades darker.

Remove the almonds from the oven and stir with a wooden spoon. Sprinkle with sel gris and set aside to cool on the baking sheet. As they cool, the sugars will begin to harden.

When the almonds have cooled, serve them in a bowl. The nuts can be stored in an airtight container for a week at room temperature.

These spicy, sweet, and salty nuts are delicious sprinkled over salads.

CORSICAN FRIED OLIVES

4 oz./115 g goats' cheese,
    at room temperature
1 teaspoon herbes de Provence
finely grated zest of 1 orange
1 egg
1 tablespoon all-purpose/plain flour
1 cup/60 g panko or coarse breadcrumbs
40 large green and black olives,
    pitted/stoned
2 cups/500 ml vegetable oil
fleur de sel, to sprinkle

*a pastry/piping bag fitted with a small
    tip/nozzle*
a deep-frying thermometer

MAKES 40

Mix together the cheese, herbs, and orange zest until smooth. Put the mixture in the pastry/piping bag and set aside.

Lightly beat the egg in a small bowl. Put the flour on a small plate and the breadcrumbs on another.

Using the pastry/piping bag, pipe each olive full with the cheese mixture. Dip each olive in the flour, then the egg, and toss in the breadcrumbs until well coated.

Heat the oil in a heavy-bottomed pan until it reaches 180°C (350°F). Alternatively, test the oil by dropping in a cube of bread. It should turn golden brown in about 20 seconds.

Fry the prepared olives in batches for about 1 minute, until crispy and golden brown. Drain on paper towels, sprinkle generously with fleur de sel, and serve.

SPICED & MARINATED OLIVES

1 dried red chile/chilli
1/4 cup/90 g Spanish salted
    Marcona almonds
1 cup/170 g green olives
3 kumquats
1/2 teaspoon cumin seeds
1/4 cup/60 ml Spanish olive oil

MAKES 2 CUPS/300 G

Roughly chop the chile/chilli and the almonds, and put them in a bowl with the olives.

Thinly slice the kumquats and add to the olive mixture. Sprinkle with cumin seeds, pour over the olive oil, and mix thoroughly.

Set aside for at least 1 hour before serving to let the flavors blend.

SALTED PRETZEL BITES

1 cup/250 ml warm water
2 tablespoons salted butter, cubed, at room temperature
3 teaspoons fast-action dried yeast
1 teaspoon white sugar
2³/₄ cups/400 g all-purpose/plain flour
4 teaspoons baking powder
rock salt flakes, for topping
American mustard, to serve (optional)

MAKES ABOUT 40

In a glass measuring pitcher/jug, mix together the warm water, butter, yeast, and sugar. Stir until the butter has melted.

To make the dough, put the flour in a food processor. With the motor running, add the liquid to the flour in a steady stream until all the liquid is incorporated and the dough forms a ball, about 3 minutes. Add a little extra flour if necessary. Put the dough on a floured worktop and knead for 2 minutes. Form into a ball and put in an oiled bowl. Cover with a kitchen cloth and let prove in a warm place for 1 hour.

Preheat the oven to 220°C (425°F) Gas 7.

Turn the dough out onto a floured worktop and roll into a 12 x 6-inch/30 x 15-cm rectangle. With a sharp knife, cut 1-inch/2.5-cm strips of dough from the long side. Take these dough strands and cut into 1-inch/2.5-cm bite-size pieces.

In a non-stick wok or large pan, add the baking powder to 4 cups/1 litre water and bring to a boil. Drop the dough pieces into the water for about 1 minute and remove with a slotted spoon onto non-stick baking sheets. They will puff up. This brining procedure gives the pretzel its slightly hard chewy outside, while the inside remains soft—much like a bagel. Sprinkle the rock salt over the pretzel bites and bake in the preheated oven for 10–15 minutes until brown on top. Serve with American mustard, if desired.

PARMESAN & SAGE WAFERS
WITH HIMALAYAN ROCK SALT

1 cup/70 g grated Parmesan cheese
1 tablespoon finely chopped fresh sage
coarse black pepper
Himalayan pink rock salt

MAKES 14

Preheat the oven to 180°C (350°F) Gas 4.

Mix together the Parmesan cheese and sage and season with black pepper. Drop tablespoons of the mixture at 2-inch/5-cm intervals onto a non-stick baking sheet. Pat down the mounds with your fingers. Bake in the preheated oven for 5–6 minutes until the mixture is completely melted and the edges are turning golden brown. Keep an eye on them as they brown fast.

Remove the wafers from the oven and let stand for a few moments to firm up. They will be soft when they come out of the oven but harden as they cool.

With a spatula, carefully remove the wafers and leave to cool completely on a wire rack. Once they have cooled, sprinkle with Himalayan pink rock salt. They can be stored in an airtight container for 2 days. These delicate lacy wafers are ideal with a glass of Prosecco, or try them instead of croutons on a Caesar salad.

HAWAIIAN BLACK SALTED BREADSTICKS

3½ cups/450 g all-purpose/
   plain flour
3 tablespoons olive oil
1 tablespoon milk
3 teaspoons fast-action dried yeast
½ teaspoon brown sugar
¼ cup/60 ml olive oil
¼ cup/110 g Hawaiian black lava
   sea salt

MAKES ABOUT 24

To make the dough, put the flour in a food processor. In a glass measuring pitcher/jug mix together 1⅓ cups/300 ml warm water, olive oil, milk, yeast, and brown sugar. With the motor running, add the liquid to the flour in a steady stream. Process until all the liquid is incorporated and the dough forms a ball, about 3 minutes. Transfer the dough to a floured worktop and knead for about 3 minutes. Form into a ball and put in an oiled bowl. Cover with a paper towel and let prove in a warm place until doubled in size.

Preheat the oven to 220°C (425°F) Gas 7.

Turn the dough out onto a floured surface. Roll into a rectangle of 15 x 10 inches/25 x 40 cm, and ¼-inch/5-mm thick. Use a sharp knife to cut ½-inch/1-cm strips of dough from the long side of the rectangle. Fold the strips in half and with the palms of your hands roll the dough into breadsticks 10 inches/25 cm long.

Arrange the breadsticks on non-stick baking sheets. Brush with the olive oil and sprinkle with the Hawaiian black lava sea salt.

Bake in the preheated oven for 10 minutes, turn the sticks over, and bake for another 10 minutes until golden. Leave to cool on a wire rack.

FISH & SEAFOOD

GREEN COCONUT SHRIMP CURRY

Delicately perfumed with kaffir lime leaves and lemongrass, this curry is given a little kick with the addition of green peppercorns and fresh chiles/chillies. Serve it up with lots of fragrant herbs and juicy limes to squeeze.

2 tablespoons coconut oil
3½ cups/820 ml coconut milk
1 cup/45 g dried unsweetened
   coconut flakes
1 lb./450 g shrimp/prawns,
   peeled, tails on
fresh cilantro/coriander, to serve
kaffir or regular limes, to serve

CURRY PASTE
2 Serrano chillies, roughly chopped
2-inch/5-cm piece of fresh ginger,
   peeled and sliced
3 stalks of lemongrass,
   white part only, sliced
3 garlic cloves
2 teaspoons green peppercorns
2 teaspoons shrimp paste
1 teaspoon ground coriander
6 kaffir lime leaves
grated zest and juice of
   1 kaffir or regular lime
2 tablespoons fish sauce

SERVES 4

Put all the ingredients for the curry paste in a blender or food processer and process until they form a paste.

Set a deep skillet/frying pan over a medium–high heat and add the coconut oil. Add the curry paste and cook for 3–4 minutes, stirring continuously. Add the coconut milk and flakes to the pan and stir to combine. Bring to a boil, then reduce the heat and simmer for 20 minutes.

Increase the heat and bring the mixture back to a boil. Add the shrimp/prawns, cover and cook for 5–6 minutes until they are pink and cooked through.

Remove from the heat and rest for 5 minutes. Spoon into bowls and sprinkle with cilantro/coriander leaves. Serve with limes to squeeze.

MACKEREL ESCABECHE WITH PICKLES

I grew up in Scotland catching mackerel off our boat, so I have a fondness for these delicious oily fish. Escabeche is a preserving technique that is widely used throughout the Mediterranean. I like making this for a weekend lunch, as it's a prepare-ahead, no-stress recipe that allows you to spend time with your friends instead of being stuck in the kitchen.

4 mackerel fillets, boned, skin on
2 tablespoons extra virgin olive oil
4 shallots, finely sliced
1 carrot, grated
2 teaspoons Tellicherry peppercorns
3 garlic cloves, finely sliced
2 bay leaves
2 teaspoons Piment d'Espelette
   or hot red pepper/chilli flakes
1½ cups/350 ml white wine
1 cup/235 ml white wine vinegar
sea salt and freshly ground
   black pepper, to taste
crusty bread, to serve

CURRIED CAULIFLOWER
2 cups/150 g cauliflower florets
1 large fennel bulb, thinly sliced
1 quantity of Basic Pickle Mix
   (p.23)
1 teaspoon curry powder
1 teaspoon mustard seeds
1 teaspoon white peppercorns

SERVES 4

You need to make the curried cauliflower at least 1 week in advance to allow the flavors to infuse. Layer the vegetables in a sterilized jar. Bring the Basic Pickle Mix to a boil, stirring to dissolve the sugar, then stir in the curry powder, mustard seeds, and peppercorns. Cook for 3 minutes, then pour into the jar and screw the lid on. Seal following the instructions on p.23.

Season the mackerel with salt and pepper, and set aside. Pour the olive oil into a medium pan over a low heat. Add the shallots, carrot, peppercorns, garlic, bay leaves, and Piment d'Espelette or hot red pepper/chilli flakes. Stir to combine and continue to cook for 3–4 minutes over a low heat, allowing the vegetables to sweat.

Increase the heat, then add the wine and vinegar, and season with a pinch of salt. Bring to a boil, then reduce to a simmer for 20 minutes.

Arrange the mackerel in the pan and spoon over some of the vegetables and juices. Cook for 3 minutes, then remove from the heat. Cover with a lid and let cool. Place the pan in the fridge for 4–24 hours.

To serve, place a fillet on each of 4 plates with a little of the juices and serve with the pickled cauliflower and some crusty bread.

CITRUS AHI TUNA WITH YUZU DIPPING SAUCE

Buy sushi-grade ahi (or yellowfin) tuna to make this dish and wrap it up in a citrusy pepper crust. The lemony yuzu juice is a must, but if you can't find it you can use lemon juice. Shiso is a wonderful citrus-flavored herb, but you could use other leaves, such as basil.

1 lb./450-g sushi-grade ahi
   (or yellowfin) tuna
2 teaspoons finely chopped
   dried orange peel
4 teaspoons ground green
   peppercorns
1 teaspoon sea salt
2 tablespoons sunflower oil
shiso leaves, to serve, optional

DIPPING SAUCE
1 tablespoon yuzu juice
2 teaspoons sesame oil
1 tablespoon soy sauce
1 teaspoon grated fresh ginger
1 teaspoon finely chopped
   green chile/chilli
a pinch of brown sugar

SERVES 2

To make the dipping sauce, whisk all the ingredients together. Pour into a bowl and set aside.

Rinse the tuna under cold running water and pat dry. Cut the tuna into two rectangles and set aside.

Mix the orange peel, peppercorns, and salt together on a large plate, then roll the tuna in the mix to completely cover.

Set a large skillet/frying pan over a medium–high heat and pour in the oil. When the pan is smoking, add the tuna and sear on all sides for about 3 minutes in total. You want the middle of the tuna to remain raw.

Transfer the tuna from the pan to a cutting board and rest for a few minutes. Place a few shiso leaves on two plates. Cut the tuna into slices 1 inch/2.5 cm thick and arrange on the leaves. Serve with the dipping sauce.

HALIBUT CEVICHE WITH CITRUS CEVICHE BRINE

I absolutely adore preparing this ceviche. The delicate brine is perfumed with lime leaves. Rub them between your hands to bruise them and release the wonderful oils from the leaves. The jewel-like tones of the lime, grapefruit, and orange slices make this dish perfect for any summer's day.

1 lb./450 g sushi-grade fresh halibut
2 shallots, finely chopped
1 pink grapefruit, peeled and very sliced thinly
1 orange, peeled and sliced very thinly
2 limes, peeled and sliced very thinly
fresh fennel pollen (see Cook's Note) and fennel flowers, to sprinkle (both optional)
1/2 teaspoon Himalayan pink salt
1/4 cup/60 ml extra virgin olive oil

CITRUS CEVICHE BRINE
6 lime leaves, bruised
grated zest and juice of 1 pink grapefruit, 1 orange, and 2 limes
1/2 teaspoon sea salt

SERVES 4–6

Rinse the halibut under cold running water and pat dry with a paper towel. Lay the fish on a wooden board and slice wafer thin.

Whisk all the Citrus Ceviche Brine ingredients together in a glass bowl. Arrange the fish in a ceramic dish in a single layer. Sprinkle over the shallots and pour over the brine, making sure all the fish is submerged in the liquid. Cover and place in the fridge for 3 hours.

After this time, remove the halibut from the fridge and arrange on a platter. Top with the citrus slices. Sprinkle with fennel pollen and flowers. Season with the salt, drizzle with the olive oil, and serve.

Cook's Note: To make your own fennel pollen, put the fresh flowers in a paper bag and leave in a cool place to dry for about 2 weeks. Shake the bag vigorously to dislodge the pollen, then remove the stems from the bag. Store the pollen in a glass jar for up to 6 months.

SALT & PEPPER SQUID WITH SANSHO SPICY DIP

This recipe, using spicy, citrusy Sansho pepper, is my spin on the ever-popular salt and pepper shrimp/prawns served in Chinese restaurants around the world. Dip the freshly fried squid into the spiced mayo and enjoy.

1/2 teaspoon ground Sansho pepper
2 teaspoons sea salt
1/2 cup/65 g rice flour
1 lb./450 g squid, cleaned and sliced
freshly squeezed juice of 1 lemon
vegetable oil, for frying

SANSHO SPICY DIP
1/2 cup/115 g good-quality mayonnaise
1/4 cup/5 g Vietnamese or regular basil leaves
1/2 teaspoon Sansho pepper
1/2 teaspoon sea salt
grated zest of 1 lemon

SERVES 4

To make the dip, whisk all the ingredients together in a small bowl until well combined. Set aside.

In a large shallow bowl mix together the Sansho pepper, salt, and rice flour. Put the squid in another bowl and pour over the lemon juice.

Pour enough oil to come halfway up a large saucepan, then place over a medium–high heat until the oil starts to simmer.

Take a few pieces of squid at a time and toss in the flour mixture to coat. Working in batches, deep fry for 2–3 minutes until golden and cooked through. Transfer to a wire rack to drain.

Pile the cooked squid in a shallow bowl and serve with the dip.

SALT COD LATKES WITH GREEN OLIVE SALSA

Here is a fun spin on bacalao, the famous Portuguese salt cod fritters.
I like to make a rich green olive salsa to pile on top. Look for green olives
marinated in herbs; they have a deep earthy taste and when combined with
the latkes bring all the flavors of the Mediterranean together. When buying
the salt cod, make sure the flesh is pure white.

1 lb./500 g salt cod
1 lb./500 g russet potatoes,
   or similar starchy potatoes
2 tablespoons fresh oregano leaves,
   roughly chopped
2 tablespoons chopped chives or
   scallions/spring onions, chopped
1 garlic clove, finely chopped
1 egg, lightly beaten
cracked black pepper, to season
olive oil, for frying

GREEN OLIVE SALSA
12 herbed green olives such
   as Picholine, pitted/stoned
1 tablespoon finely grated
   lemon zest
2 tablespoons olive oil

MAKES 24

Put the salt cod in a bowl and cover with cold water.
Place in the fridge for 2 days, changing the water
4 times a day. This will rehydrate the cod and remove
any excess salt.

When the cod is ready, drain, put in a pot, and
cover with cold water. Bring to a boil and cook for
15 minutes until the cod begins to break away from
the skin and bones. Remove from the heat, drain,
and cool. Using a fork, flake the fish, discarding
the skin and bones. Mash and set aside.

Peel and roughly grate the potatoes. In a large bowl
mix together the cod, potatoes, oregano, chive onions
or scallions/spring onions, garlic, and egg. Season
with black pepper and set aside.

To make the green olive salsa, roughly chop the
herbed green olives and put in a small bowl. Add the
lemon zest along with the olive oil and mix thoroughly.

Preheat a medium-size non-stick sauté pan over a
medium to high heat and drizzle with enough olive
oil to fry the latkes. Drop heaping tablespoons of the
latke mixture into the pan.

Cook the latkes for 2–3 minutes on each side until
crispy and golden brown, and the potato is cooked.
Repeat in batches until you have used all the mixture.

Arrange the latkes on a serving plate, top with a little
salsa, and serve.

SALT-CRUSTED CITRUS SHRIMP
WITH SPICY DIPPING SAUCE

This is a showstopper at any dinner party. Crack open the salt crust at the table and let your guests be dazzled by the heavenly aromas and the bright pink shells of these delightful sea creatures.

finely grated zest and freshly
    squeezed juice of 2 limes
4 lbs./1.8 kg coarse sea salt
1 lb./450 g large shrimp/prawns,
    unshelled

SPICY DIPPING SAUCE
2 red chiles/chillies, finely chopped
4 kaffir lime leaves, finely shredded
1 scallion/spring onion, finely
    chopped
1 garlic clove, finely chopped
1/2 cup/125 ml fish sauce
finely grated zest and freshly
    squeezed juice of 2 limes
1 tablespoon rice wine vinegar
1 tablespoon brown sugar
1 tablespoon peanuts, chopped

SERVES 4

Preheat the oven to 240°C (475°F) Gas 9.

In a large bowl mix together the lime zest and juice, salt, and 1 cup/250 ml water. The mixture should be the consistency of wet sand. Spread a layer of the salt mixture in a baking dish and arrange the shrimp/prawns on top. Cover with the remaining salt mixture and pat down well, making sure the shrimp/prawns are completely covered and there are no gaps.

Bake in the preheated oven for 15 minutes. The salt should be slightly golden on top.

Whisk together all the spicy dipping sauce ingredients until the sugar has dissolved. Divide between small bowls.

When the shrimp/prawns are ready, take them out of the oven and let them rest for 5 minutes. Using the back of a knife, crack open the crust and remove the top part. Serve at the table.

Let guests help themselves, peel their own shrimp/prawns, and dip in the spicy sauce. Have a large empty bowl handy for the shells and plenty of napkins.

MISO & NUT-CRUSTED SALMON

Miso is a traditional staple of Japanese cooking. It is made by fermenting soybeans in sea salt, which results in a thick paste. Most common are white, yellow, and red miso pastes. The delicate, slightly salty, and fruity taste of yellow miso really enhances the flavor of wild salmon. This is a fantastic easy supper dish and healthy, too.

2 x 8-oz./225-g wild salmon fillets
1 tablespoon olive oil
chopped fresh chive onions,
    to garnish
lemon wedges, to serve

MISO & NUT TOPPING
1 tablespoon yellow miso paste
1/2 cup/60 g cashews,
    roughly chopped
1/2 red Serrano chile/chilli,
    finely chopped
finely grated zest and freshly
    squeezed juice of 1 lime
1 tablespoon toasted sesame oil

SERVES 2

Preheat the oven to 200°C (400°F) Gas 6.

Rinse the salmon under cold running water and dry on paper towels. Drizzle the olive oil into a small baking dish and place the salmon fillets in it.

To make the miso and nut topping, mix together the miso, cashews, chile/chilli, lime zest and juice, and sesame oil. Divide the mixture and spread on top of the salmon fillets.

Cook in the preheated oven for 12–15 minutes until the fish is cooked and the topping is golden brown.

Garnish with chopped chive onions and serve with lemon wedges.

SALT-CURED GRAVADLAX WITH CAPER SAUCE

It seems everyone has a favorite way of making this classic dish. My overnight version is quick compared with the traditional method of curing for several days. Wild salmon makes a huge difference; if it's not available, use organic farmed salmon. The gravadlax will keep for 5 days in the fridge.

2¹/2 lbs./1.1 kg wild salmon fillet,
    boned and with skin on
    (this is 1 side of a whole salmon)
2 tablespoons juniper berries
2 tablespoons black peppercorns,
    crushed
1 cup/110 g coarse sea salt
¹/2 cup/225 g brown sugar
3 bunches fresh dill
¹/4 cup/60 ml gin
lemon wedges and baguette slices,
    to serve

CAPER SAUCE
1 cup/225 g crème fraîche
2 tablespoons salt
2 tablespoons cornichons
1 tablespoon salted capers
finely grated zest and freshly
    squeezed juice of 1 lemon

a prepared baking sheet or dish
    (see method)

SERVES 8

You will need a baking sheet or shallow dish that will accommodate the whole salmon. Line the bottom of this with plastic wrap/clingfilm.

Crush the juniper berries and black peppercorns using a mortar and pestle.

In a bowl mix together the sea salt and brown sugar with the crushed peppercorns and juniper berries. Sprinkle half the salt mixture on top of the prepared baking sheet or dish and spread one of the bunches of dill over the salt mixture. Place the salmon, skin-side down, on top of the dill and drizzle with the gin. Cover the salmon with the remainder of the salt mixture and then top with the remaining dill.

Cover the salmon with plastic wrap/clingfilm, making sure it is airtight. Next, you need to put a weight on the salmon; a heavy saucepan or pizza stone is ideal. Put the salmon in the fridge overnight to cure for 12 hours.

To make the caper sauce, put all the ingredients in a food processor and pulse until roughly chopped. Transfer to a bowl, cover, and refrigerate.

Unwrap the salmon and remove the dill. Place the salmon on a wooden board. Using the back of a knife, scrape off the salt mixture.

To serve, cut the salmon as thinly as possible in diagonal slices. Serve with the caper sauce, lemon wedges, and a crusty baguette.

SALT-CRUSTED BRANZINO

Branzino is also known as Mediterranean sea bass. It is a white flaky fish with a sweetish taste. You could use any firm fish for this recipe. I like to include fennel seeds in the crust to add an extra layer of flavor.

1 whole branzino, about
   2 lbs./900 g, cleaned
2 sprigs of fresh rosemary
1 lemon, sliced, plus wedges
   to serve
1/2 fennel bulb, thinly sliced
1 garlic clove, thinly sliced
1/4 cup/60 ml white wine
5 egg whites
6 cups/1.4 kg coarse sea salt
   or rock salt
4 tablespoons fennel seeds
cracked black pepper, to season

SERVES 2

Preheat the oven to 220°C (425°F) Gas 7.

Wash the fish under cold running water and pat dry with paper towels. Stuff the fish with the rosemary, lemon slices, fennel, and garlic. Drizzle with the white wine.

In a large bowl, lightly whisk the egg whites. Add the salt and fennel seeds and mix until it is the consistency of wet sand. Spread half the salt mixture in the bottom of a baking dish and lay the fish on top. Season with cracked black pepper. Cover the fish with the remainder of the salt and pack tightly, making sure there are no holes for the steam to escape.

Bake in the preheated oven for 30 minutes, then remove and allow the fish to rest untouched for another 5 minutes. Crack open the salt crust with the back of a knife and remove the salt from around the fish.

Serve with lemon wedges.

MEAT & POULTRY

PEPPERED BEEF PHO

The thing I love most about pho is all the sauces and herbs that go along with it. You can make a simple bowl or go to town and really dress it up—there are no rules!

6 cups/1.5 litres good-quality chicken stock

2 star anise

1-inch/2.5-cm piece of fresh ginger

2 tablespoons fish sauce

2 tablespoons toasted sesame oil

3 tablespoons soy sauce

1 tablespoon sambal oelek (Asian chile/chilli paste)

1 teaspoon Lampong peppercorns, cracked

1 garlic clove, finely chopped

1 lb./450 g sirloin steak

4 cups/600 g cooked rice noodles

2 cups/115 g beansprouts

1 cup/135 g grated carrot

3 scallions/spring onions, finely sliced

2 red chiles/chillies, finely sliced

selection of fresh Vietnamese basil, mint, cilantro/coriander, lime wedges, and chili/chilli sauce, to serve

SERVES 4

Pour the chicken stock into a saucepan and add the star anise, ginger, and fish sauce. Bring to a boil, then reduce the heat and simmer for 20 minutes.

In a shallow bowl whisk together the sesame oil, soy sauce, sambal oelek, peppercorns and garlic. Add the steak and coat with the marinade.

Set a heavy-based cast-iron skillet/frying pan over a high heat until smoking.

Add the steak and sear for 2 minutes on each side, then transfer to a cutting board. Reduce the heat and add the remainder of the marinade to the pan.

Cook for a few minutes until thickened, then pour into a small bowl. Slice the steak into thin strips.

Divide the noodles, beansprouts, and grated carrot into four large bowls. Top with strips of steak and pour over the hot broth. Sprinkle with the scallions/spring onions and chiles/chillies. Serve with the fresh herbs, lime wedges, and sauce.

PEPPER-CRUSTED STEAK WITH DRAMBUIE SAUCE

Drambuie hails from Scotland and is made from whisky infused with spices, heather honey, and herbs. It is believed to be a recipe created for Bonnie Prince Charlie. Lacing it through a pepper sauce adds wonderful warmth, and it is especially good with steak.

1½ lb./680 g Porterhouse or T-bone steak, 1½ inches/3.5 cm thick
1 tablespoon fresh thyme leaves, plus a few stalks to garnish
2 tablespoons olive oil
4 teaspoons cracked rainbow peppercorns
2 tablespoons/30 g salted butter
1 shallot, finely diced
1 garlic clove, finely chopped
½ cup/120 ml heavy/double cream
½ cup/120 ml beef stock
4 tablespoons Drambuie
sea salt, to taste

SERVES 2

Put the steak in a ceramic dish and season with salt. Mix together the thyme, half the olive oil, and 3 teaspoons of the peppercorns and spread over the steak to make a crust.

Set a heavy-based cast-iron pan over a high heat until smoking, then add the steak. Cook for 8 minutes, then turn over, reduce the heat to medium, and cook for a further 5 minutes. Transfer the steak to a warm plate, cover with foil, and rest for 10 minutes.

Add the remaining olive oil to the pan along with the butter and stir to melt. Add the remaining peppercorns, shallot, and garlic, and stir. Cook for 4–5 minutes over a medium heat until golden brown. Stir in the cream, stock, and Drambuie and bring to a boil, then reduce the heat and simmer for a few minutes. Season with salt and pour into a small pitcher/jug.

Slice the steak, garnish with the thyme stalks, and serve with the sauce.

INDIAN PEPPER CHICKEN

I love making curries, partly due to all the beautifully colored ingredients that go into them. This curry is laced with spicy and aromatic crushed Malabar peppercorns from India's south-west coast. Dried fruit adds a touch of sweetness to the dish.

8 chicken thighs, skin on, bone in
2 teaspoons ground Malabar
   pepper
1 teaspoon sea salt
4 tablespoons ghee or olive oil
1 large onion, diced
2 garlic cloves, finely chopped
1 teaspoon curry powder
1 teaspoon turmeric
1 teaspoon ancho chilli powder
1 teaspoon ground cumin
4 sprigs of fresh curry leaves
475 ml/2 cups chicken stock
70 g/½ cup raisins or dried dates
naan bread, to serve

SERVES 4

Sprinkle the chicken thighs with the pepper and salt, making sure they are completely coated.

Set a large skillet/frying pan over a medium–high heat and add 3 tablespoons of the ghee or oil. Put the chicken skin-side down in the pan and sauté for about 4 minutes, until golden brown. Turn the chicken over and brown the other side, then transfer to a large plate.

Add the remaining ghee or oil to the pan, and add the onion and garlic and cook until golden brown (about 5 minutes). Add the curry powder, turmeric, chili/chilli powder and cumin, and stir to combine. Cook for about 2 minutes.

Return the chicken to the pan, skin-side down, and top with the curry leaves. Pour over the chicken stock and bring to a boil, then reduce the heat to a simmer and cover the pan with a lid or foil. Cook for 30 minutes.

Remove the lid and toss in the raisins or dates. Turn the chicken thighs over and continue to cook uncovered for another 30 minutes.

Serve the chicken with the sauce and warm naan bread.

CHICKEN AU POIVRE

Roast chicken is one of my favorite dinners, and cooking it with a lovely layer of briny green peppercorn butter makes it even better. A play on the classic steak au poivre, it is delicious.

4 tablespoons/60 g butter,
    at room temperature
2 tablespoons brined green
    peppercorns
grated zest of 1 lemon
2 tablespoons lemon juice
1 teaspoon sea salt,
    plus extra to season
4 lbs./1.8 kg chicken
olive oil, to drizzle
1 head of garlic, cut in half
a few sprigs of fresh thyme
1/4 cup/60 ml white wine

SAUCE
1 tablespoon brined green
    peppercorns
1 shallot, sliced
1 cup/240 ml white wine
1 cup/240 ml heavy/double cream

SERVES 4

Preheat the oven to 190°C (375°F) Gas 5.

Put the butter, peppercorns, lemon zest and juice, and salt in a food processor and process until combined.

Put the chicken in a roasting pan. Using a knife, make a pocket between the skin and the flesh on the chicken breast and stuff with the pepper butter. Smooth out with your hands, making sure the butter is evenly distributed.

Rub any leftover butter over the top of the chicken, then drizzle with olive oil and sprinkle with sea salt.

Add the garlic and sprigs of thyme to the pan and pour in the wine. Roast in the preheated oven for 1 hour, then remove from the oven. Spoon 4 tablespoons of the cooking juices into a skillet/frying pan for the sauce. Cover the chicken with foil and rest for 15 minutes.

To make the sauce, set the skillet/frying pan over a medium–high heat and add the peppercorns and shallot to the cooking juices. Take one of the roasted garlic halves and squeeze the garlic into the pan. Cook for 3 minutes, squashing the garlic down to a paste. Add the wine and cream and bring to a boil, then reduce the heat to a lively simmer. Season with salt and cook for 10 minutes, stirring occasionally. Pour into a pitcher/jug and serve alongside the chicken.

SZECHUAN ROASTED PORK BELLY WITH PLUMS

Pork belly is one of my all-time favorites. Slowly roast it to a dark, crispy crust and then top with sweet, juicy plums. In winter serve it with noodles or rice, and in summer keep it simple with a large, crisp green salad. Allow plenty of marinating time for the best flavor.

a 3¹/₂-lb./1.5-kg piece of pork belly
2 teaspoons sea salt
¹/₄ cup/70 g orange-blossom honey
¹/₄ cup/60 ml soy sauce
¹/₄ cup/60 ml rice wine vinegar
1 tablespoon toasted sesame oil
1 tablespoon sambal oelek
   (Asian chile/chilli paste)
1 tablespoon crushed Szechuan
   peppercorns
4 garlic cloves
a 2-inch/5-cm piece of fresh ginger,
   peeled
¹/₂ teaspoon ground cinnamon
6 medium plums, halved and pitted

SERVES 6

Put the pork belly on a worksurface. Score the skin and rub all over with the salt.

Put the honey, soy sauce, vinegar, sesame oil, sambal oelek, peppercorns, garlic, ginger, and cinnamon in a blender and process until smooth. Pour the mixture into a baking dish and lay the pork on top, skin-side down. Spoon the mixture over the pork to coat evenly. Cover and refrigerate for 6–24 hours.

Remove the pork from the fridge, uncover, and bring to room temperature.

Preheat the oven to 175°C (350°F) Gas 4.

Place the pork in the oven and roast for 2 hours, basting every 30 minutes.

Remove the pork from the oven and drain off the excess fat. Turn the pork skin-side up in the pan so that it crisps. Arrange the plums around the pork and return to the oven for 30–40 minutes. Remove from the oven and tent with foil. Rest for 15 minutes.

To serve, cut into thick slices and top with the roasted plums.

KOREAN STICKY RIBS
WITH PICKLED CARROT & RAISINS

Gochujang is a red pepper paste used in Korean cooking. It comes in varying degrees of heat, so check the label and choose something to suit your own tastebuds. Serve with the Pickled Carrots & Raisins or an Asian slaw.

8 Korean-style beef ribs, each
  1 cm/¹/₂ inch thick
3 spring onions/scallions, thinly
  sliced
2 tablespoons black sesame seeds

MARINADE
60 ml/¹/₄ cup soy sauce
60 ml/¹/₄ cup toasted sesame oil
140 g/¹/₂ cup orange-blossom honey
2 heaping tablespoons gochujang
1 tablespoon fish sauce
4 garlic cloves, bashed
2 Serrano chiles/chillies, chopped
2 teaspoons cracked rainbow
  peppercorns
¹/₂ teaspoon sea salt

PICKLED CARROT & RAISINS
6 carrots, grated
100 g/³/₄ cup raisins
2 shallots, thinly sliced
1 teaspoon Lampong peppercorns,
  coarsely chopped
1 quantity of Basic Pickle Mix (p.23)
¹/₂ teaspoon ground cumin
¹/₂ teaspoon ground coriander

SERVES 4

Lay the ribs in a single layer in a ceramic baking dish.

Put all the marinade ingredients in a blender and process until smooth. Pour over the ribs and sprinkle with the scallions/spring onions and sesame seeds. Cover and refrigerate for 6–24 hours.

Remove the ribs from the fridge and bring to room temperature. Heat a grill/broiler or barbecue to a medium–high heat. Place the ribs on the rack and cook for 5 minutes, then turn over and cook for another 5 minutes. Transfer to a warm plate and tent with foil. Rest for 10 minutes.

Put the remaining marinade in a small saucepan and bring to a boil, then reduce the heat and simmer for 5 minutes. To serve, pour the marinade into a bowl and serve alongside the ribs.

For the Pickled Carrot & Raisin This pickle needs to be made at least 1 week in advance to allow the flavors to infuse. Layer the carrot, raisins, shallots, and peppercorns in a sterilized jar. Bring the Basic Pickle Mix to the boil, then add the cumin and coriander, and stir to dissolve the sugar. Cook for 3 minutes, then pour into the jar and screw the lid on. Seal following the instructions on p.23.

CRISPY ROAST DUCK & ASIAN GREENS
WITH GREEN TEA SALT

Rubbing kosher salt over the duck draws excess moisture out of the skin, while scalding makes for a crispy skin when roasted. A wonderful spiced honey glaze adds a vibrant color and flavor to the meat.

1 fresh duck, 3 lbs./1.4 kg
3 tablespoons kosher salt

HONEY GLAZE
4 star anise, crushed
1/3 cup/100 ml honey
1 teaspoon ground cinnamon
finely grated zest of 1 orange
  and freshly squeezed juice of
  1/2 orange (halves reserved)
1 teaspoon Sichuan crushed
  peppercorns
2 tablespoons soy sauce
a 1-inch/2.5-cm piece of fresh
  ginger, peeled and grated
2 red Thai chiles/chillies, chopped
2 tablespoons dark brown sugar

ASIAN GREENS
3 tablespoons peanut oil
2 tablespoons toasted sesame oil
2 tablespoons red wine vinegar
1 teaspoon soy sauce
1 teaspoon honey
3 cups/350 g mixed Asian salad
  greens
cracked black pepper and
  green tea salt

a roasting pan lined with foil
a roasting rack

SERVES 4

Wash and dry the duck. Rub the kosher salt all over the duck skin, cover, and leave in the fridge overnight.

Put the roasting rack in the lined roasting pan. Bring a kettle of water to a boil. Put the duck in a large bowl and pour boiling water over it. Immediately remove the duck from the bowl and place on the rack. Set aside.

Preheat the oven to 200°C (400°F) Gas 6.

Stuff the duck with the reserved orange halves. Mix all the honey glaze ingredients together in a bowl and brush over the duck. Roast in the preheated oven for 30 minutes, remove from the oven, and drain off the fat that has accumulated in the bottom of the pan. You may need to cover the tips of the wings with foil, as they will be very crispy. Turn the oven down to 190°C (375°F) Gas 5 and put the duck back in the oven for another 30 minutes.

Remove the duck from the oven and let it rest for 15 minutes in a warm place.

To prepare the Asian greens, whisk the peanut oil, sesame oil, red wine vinegar, soy sauce, and honey together. Season with cracked black pepper and green tea salt. Put the salad greens in a bowl and toss with the dressing.

Carve the duck and serve with the salad.

JASMINE-BRINED ROASTED POUSSINS
WITH SALSA VERDE

Brining the poussins ensures a crispy skin when roasted. You can use any tea to make the brine, but jasmine tea infuses a floral taste into the poussins and creates a subtle flavor when cooked. Serve with the dark green salsa verde. You can also make this with Cornish game hen.

2 poussins (or 1 Cornish game
  hen), weighing 1½ lbs./700 g
1 small unwaxed lemon
1 garlic clove, crushed
1 tablespoon olive oil
sea salt and cracked black pepper,
  to season

BRINING SOLUTION
4 tablespoons jasmine tea
  or 4 jasmine teabags
6 cups/1.5 litres boiling water
¼ cup/60 g coarse rock salt
1 tablespoon dark brown sugar

SALSA VERDE
1 cup/20 g fresh Italian parsley
1 cup/20 g fresh cilantro/coriander
1 cup/20 g fresh mint
2 garlic cloves, finely chopped
zest of 1 small unwaxed lemon
1 tablespoon brined capers
½ cup/125 ml olive oil

a roasting pan

kitchen twine

SERVES 2

First make the brine. Put the jasmine tea in a large measuring jug/pitcher and pour over the boiling water. Add the rock salt and dark brown sugar and stir until dissolved. Set aside to cool completely.

Wash and dry the poussins and put in a deep dish. Pour the cooled brine over them, cover, and refrigerate for 6–8 hours.

When you are ready to cook, preheat the oven to 190°C (375°F) Gas 5. Remove the poussins from the brining mixture and pat dry, removing any leftover tea leaves. Discard the brining mixture; it cannot be used again.

Place the poussins in a roasting pan. Zest the lemon and reserve for use in the salsa verde. Cut the lemon into quarters and stuff the cavities with them. Tie the legs together with kitchen twine. Mix together the garlic and oil, and rub over the skin of the poussins. Season with sea salt and cracked black pepper. Roast in the preheated oven for 35 minutes until cooked and the poussin juices run clear.

To make the salsa verde, put all the salsa ingredients in a food processor and pulse until roughly chopped. Be careful not to overprocess; you want the salsa to be slightly chunky. Season with sea salt and black pepper.

When the poussins are ready, remove from the oven and set aside to rest for 10 minutes, covered with foil, in a warm place. Carve and serve with the salsa verde.

MUSTARD & HERB CHICKEN BAKED IN A SALT CRUST

This chicken dish is so easy to prepare. You will be amazed at how beautifully succulent it is, as the salt crust keeps all the moisture in during cooking. As you are using egg whites to help bind the salt, save the yolks and make aïoli or mayonnaise to go with cold leftovers.

1 chicken, 3¹/₂–4 lbs./1.5–1.8 kg
1 lemon, cut in half
3 tablespoons Dijon mustard
1 tablespoon herbes de Provence
5 egg whites
4 lbs./1.8 kg coarse sea salt
cracked black pepper, to season

*a roasting pan or baking dish
   similar in size to the chicken*

SERVES 6

Preheat the oven to 190°C (375°F) Gas 5.

Stuff the chicken with the lemon halves and rub the mustard all over the skin. Sprinkle with the herbes de Provence and season with cracked black pepper. Set the chicken aside.

In a large bowl lightly beat the egg whites until frothy. Add the salt and mix thoroughly. The mixture should be the consistency of wet sand.

Spread a thin layer of the salt mixture evenly on the bottom of the roasting pan or baking dish. Put the chicken on top and cover with the rest of the salt mixture. Pat down well and make sure there are no holes through which the steam can escape.

Bake the chicken in the preheated oven for 1 hour. You'll notice that the salt will turn a golden brown. Remove the chicken from the oven and let it rest for 10 minutes.

Using the back of a knife, crack open the crust and remove the chicken. Transfer to a plate or wooden board and carve.

INDIAN-SPICED LEG OF LAMB
COOKED IN A SALT CRUST WITH RAITA

This is a simple way to cook lamb—coat it in a thick crust and roast it in the oven. The aromas from the spices are intoxicating, especially the fresh curry leaves hidden in the crust.

3 lb./1.3 kg leg of lamb, bone in
4 garlic cloves, sliced

SPICE RUB
20 green cardamom pods, bashed
1 teaspoon cumin seeds
1 cinnamon stick, broken into pieces
1/2 teaspoon each of whole cloves, turmeric, chipotle powder, and Spanish smoked paprika
2 tablespoons olive oil

SALT CRUST
2 1/2 cups/550 g coarse sea salt
3 1/2 cups/450 g all-purpose/plain flour
1 small bunch fresh curry leaves

RAITA
1 cup/225 ml plain yogurt
2 garlic cloves, finely chopped
1 small cucumber, grated
2 tablespoons fresh mint leaves, torn
sea salt, to season
ground sumac, to sprinkle

SERVES 6–8

Wash the leg of lamb and pat dry with paper towels. Using a sharp knife, stab the lamb all over and stud with the slices of garlic. Set aside.

Put all the dry ingredients for the spice rub in a saucepan and dry roast over a low heat, stirring continuously until they are lightly toasted. Pound the toasted spices to a rough mixture using a mortar and pestle. Add the olive oil and stir to a paste. Spread the paste all over the lamb and chill in the fridge for at least 2 hours or for up to 24 hours.

When you are ready to cook the lamb, preheat the oven to 200°C (400°F) Gas 6.

To make the salt crust, mix the salt, flour, and curry leaves together in a bowl with 1 cup/250 ml water to give a doughy consistency. If the mixture is too dry, add more water 1 tablespoon at a time. Roll out on a floured worktop to twice the size of the lamb. Put the lamb leg at one end of the pastry and fold over the remaining dough. Seal, making sure there are no holes for any steam to escape. Put in a lightly oiled roasting pan and bake in the preheated oven for 1 hour.

Take the lamb out of the oven and let rest for 10–15 minutes.

To make the raita, mix together the yogurt, garlic, grated cucumber, and mint leaves. Season with sea salt and sprinkle with the sumac.

To serve the lamb, peel off the crust and place on a large plate or wooden board to carve. Serve with the raita.

LAVENDER SALT-CRUSTED LEG OF LAMB

Salt rubs are a fantastic way to get flavor into food. There are several varieties of lavender and all are good to cook with. The dainty flowers release wonderful oils, which are filled with flavor. For some reason, lavender and lamb just go together. I have given two salt rub options here, the second option features pink salt and includes dried Provençal herbs.

a 4-lb./1.8-kg leg of lamb, bone in
6 garlic cloves, sliced
leaves from 2 fresh sprigs of
   rosemary
olive oil, to drizzle

LAVENDER SEA SALT RUB
4 generous tablespoons dried
   culinary lavender
2 tablespoons good-quality coarse
   sea salt
1 teaspoon ground black pepper

**PINK SALT HERBES DE
PROVENCE RUB**
2 tablespoons each dried thyme,
   dried rosemary, dried basil,
   fennel seeds, dried winter savory
2 tablespoons Murray River pink
   salt flakes
3 tablespoons dried culinary
   lavender flowers

SERVES 6

Preheat the oven to 425°F (220°C) Gas 7.

Rinse the lamb under cold running water and pat dry with a paper towel. Put the leg in a roasting pan and with a sharp knife make shallow incisions over the lamb. Stud with the garlic and rosemary. Rub your choice of lavender salt mixture all over the lamb and drizzle with the olive oil.

Roast the lamb in the preheated oven for 15 minutes, then turn down the temperature to 350°F (180°C) Gas 4 and roast for a further 45 minutes. The lamb will be pink in the middle. If you prefer your lamb medium to well done, cook for a further 15 minutes.

Remove the lamb from the oven, cover loosely with kitchen foil, and let rest for 15 minutes before carving.

For both the salt rubs Put all the ingredients in a bowl and mix together.

Store the rub in a glass jar with a tight-fitting lid for up to 6 months. The rubs can also be used on chicken and fish or sprinkled as a finishing salt.

MINT & LEMON THYME LAMB KABOBS
WITH QUICK PICKLED CUKES

I like to use lamb shoulder for these kabobs/kebabs as it holds up well
on a hot grill and marinating overnight helps to tenderize the meat.

1¹/₂ lbs./680 g lamb shoulder,
  chilled
1 lemon
6 fresh bay leaves
cracked black pepper

MINT & LEMON THYME RUB
¹/₂ preseved lemon, finely chopped
1 tablespoon dried mint
2 tablespoons fresh lemon thyme
  leaves
1 tablespoon fresh rosemary leaves
¹/₄ cup/60 ml extra virgin olive oil
grated zest and freshly squeezed
  juice of 1 lemon
sea salt and cracked black pepper

6 x 12-inch/30-cm wooden skewers,
  soaked in cold water before use
  (or sprigs of rosemary as shown)

QUICK PICKLED CUKES
1 lb./450 g pickling cucumbers
1 tablespoon Kosher/table salt
2 teaspoons brown sugar
¹/₂ teaspoon black peppercorns
¹/₂ teaspoon pink peppercorns
1 teaspoon yellow mustard seeds
4 fresh bay leaves
1¹/₂ cups/350 ml apple cider
  vinegar

1 sterilized quart/litre glass jar
  with lid

SERVES 6

Rinse the lamb under cold running water and pat dry
with a paper towel. Cut the lamb into1¼-inch/3-cm
cubes and put in a mixing bowl.

Put all of the Mint and Lemon Thyme Rub ingredients
in a bowl and mix together. Rub it over the lamb and toss
to coat evenly. Season with cracked black pepper. Cover
and refrigerate for 8–24 hours.

Slice the lemon in half, then cut each half into half moons.

Remove the lamb from the fridge and, while still cold,
thread onto the prepared skewers (or rosemary sprigs)
along with the bay leaves and lemon slices. Cover and
allow to come to room temperature.

On a medium–high grill/barbecue, cook the skewers
for 5 minutes, then reduce the heat to medium and turn
them over. Cook for 6–8 minutes more, turning often
to make sure all the sides are brown and crispy.

For the Quick Pickled Cukes Cut the cucumbers
into spears and pack them into the glass jar.

In a non-reactive pan, add the salt, sugar, peppercorns,
mustard seeds, bay leaves, cider vinegar, and ¹/₄ cup/
60 ml water. Bring to a boil over a medium–high heat,
then reduce the heat to medium and simmer until the
salt and sugar have dissolved. Pour the hot pickling juice
over the cucumbers and fill to the top. Screw the lid
on and allow to cool completely before placing in the
refrigerator. These pickles will keep for up to 2 weeks.

1 lb./450 g pork tenderloin
lime wedges and cilantro/coriander,
    to serve (optional)

SPICY MARINADE
2 tablespoons rice wine vinegar
2 green chiles/chillies, chopped
1 tablespoon Kecap Manis
    (thick medium-sweet soy sauce)
1 large garlic clove, finely chopped
1 tablespoon toasted sesame oil
2 tablespoons fish sauce
2 tablespoons peanut oil
2 tablespoons chopped cilantro/
    coriander leaves
1 tablespoon grated fresh ginger

ROAST SALTED PEANUT SAUCE
1 tablespoon peanut oil
1 garlic clove, finely chopped
2 red Thai chiles/chillies,
    finely chopped
4 kaffir lime leaves
1 stalk lemongrass, cut into 4
1 teaspoon garam masala
    or curry powder
2 tablespoons dark brown sugar
1 cup/225 g Salty Peanut Butter
    (see p.27)
1 cup/250 ml coconut milk
1/4 cup/30 g unsweetened
    shredded/dessicated coconut
finely grated zest and freshly
    squeezed juice of 1 lime
2 tablespoons fish sauce

*18–20 small metal skewers or
    bamboo soaked in cold water
    for 30 minutes*

MAKES 18–20

SPICY PORK SATAY SKEWERS
WITH ROAST SALTED PEANUT SAUCE

These spicy pork skewers dipped in peanut sauce are heaven on a stick. They are great for weekend get-togethers, when you want to make delicious, easy food with minimum kitchen time. You can also pop these on a barbecue grill and forgo the stovetop.

Slice the pork into 1/4-inch/5-mm pieces and put in a bowl. Mix together all the spicy marinade ingredients and pour over the pork. Cover and put in the fridge for 30 minutes.

To make the roast salted peanut sauce, heat the peanut oil in a saucepan over medium heat. Sauté the garlic, chiles/chillies, kaffir lime leaves, lemongrass, and garam masala for 2 minutes. Add the sugar and stir. Now add the Salty Peanut Butter, coconut milk, shredded/dessicated coconut, and the lime zest and juice. Cook for 15 minutes. Take off the heat and stir in the fish sauce. Pour the mixture into a bowl and set aside.

Remove the pork pieces from the fridge and thread onto the skewers.

Heat a grill pan/cast iron skillet over high heat until nearly smoking. Cook the pork skewers for 3–4 minutes each side until brown and caramelized.

Garnish the pork skewers with cilantro/coriander leaves and serve with lime wedges and the Roast Salted Peanut Sauce.

VEGETARIAN DISHES

SPICY MAPLE BAKED TOFU
WITH BUCKWHEAT NOODLES

I love the slight sweetness of the maple syrup combined with the earthiness of the spice, then topped with a breath of the ocean with nori seaweed. Serve the tofu warm or chilled—either way it's heaven in a bowl.

1 lb./450 g firm organic tofu
1/3 cup/70 ml good-quality
    maple syrup
1 tablespoon olive oil
2 teaspoons smoked pimentón
1 teaspoon freshly cracked
    Tellicherry pepper
a pinch of sea salt
9 1/2 oz./270 g buckwheat
    soba noodles
tamari or soy sauce, to drizzle
1 sheet of nori seaweed, crumbled
    or finely sliced

SERVES 4

Preheat the oven to 200°C (400°F) Gas 6.

Slice the tofu into pieces 1/2 inch/1 cm thick and arrange in a single layer in a ceramic baking dish.

In a medium bowl whisk together the maple syrup, olive oil, smoked pimentón, pepper, and sea salt. Pour over the tofu to coat, then bake in the preheated oven for 30 minutes.

Bring a large pan of water to a boil over a high heat and add the noodles. Cook for 4 minutes, then drain, rinse under cold water, and set aside.

To serve, divide the noodles between four bowls and drizzle with a touch of tamari or soy sauce. Top with a couple of pieces of tofu and sprinkle with a little of the seaweed.

LEMON PEPPER RICOTTA GNOCCHI

A wonderful artisanal gnocchi that you will make over and over again. The flavors are gentle and fresh with a little kick from the pepper. Dusted in lashings of Parmesan and drizzled with good olive oil and fresh lemon, it is a perfect dish all year round, as a simple spring supper or a hearty dinner served alongside short ribs or stews.

2 cups/50 g ricotta
grated zest of 2 large lemons
1/4 cup/20 g freshly grated Parmesan cheese, plus extra to serve
3/4 cup/100 g all-purpose/plain flour, plus extra for dusting
1 large egg, beaten
1/2 teaspoon ground white pepper, plus extra for dusting
1/2 teaspoon sea salt
extra virgin olive oil
1/2 cup/20 g torn mixed fresh green herbs of your choice

SERVES 4–6

In a large bowl mix the ricotta, half the lemon zest, Parmesan, flour, egg, pepper, and salt until well combined.

Turn out onto a worksurface lightly dusted with flour and roll into a ball. Divide into four pieces. Taking one piece at a time, roll into a thin sausage shape. Repeat with the other pieces. Using a sharp knife, cut the dough into pieces 1 inch/2.5 cm long.

Bring a large pasta pot of salted water to a boil. Add the gnocchi and cook for a few minutes. They will float to the surface when cooked.

Drain and toss into a large bowl. Drizzle liberally with olive oil and add the remaining lemon zest, extra Parmesan, and the herbs. Toss and serve in bowls with a dusting of white pepper to finish.

OLIVE SUPPLI WITH SAFFRON SALT

Traditional suppli have mozzarella inside and are known in Rome as suppli al telefono, because when you bite into them the mozzarella pulls and looks like a telephone wire. I hide a cured black olive in the center of mine, which makes for a delicious surprise.

16 cured black olives, pitted/stoned
1/4 cup/40 g all-purpose/plain flour
2 eggs, beaten
1½ cups/140 g breadcrumbs
vegetable oil, for frying
saffron salt, to sprinkle

RISOTTO
1/2 cup/20 g dried porcini
　mushrooms
1 cup/250 ml white wine
2 cups/500 ml chicken stock
2 tablespoons olive oil
1 garlic clove, finely chopped
2 tablespoons fresh thyme leaves
1 tablespoon chopped fresh
　rosemary
1 cup/200 g arborio rice
1/2 cup/60 g grated Parmesan
　cheese
cracked black pepper and sea salt

a deep-frying thermometer

MAKES 16

For the risotto, soak the mushrooms in the wine for 30 minutes. Drain, reserving the liquid, and chop roughly. Pour the reserved liquid into a small pan with the chicken stock. Bring to a boil, then reduce to a simmer.

Put the olive oil, garlic, thyme, rosemary, and mushrooms in a medium pan and cook over medium to high heat for a few seconds, coating with the olive oil. Add the rice and stir for 2–3 minutes until well coated and translucent. Start adding the stock a ladleful at a time, stirring continuously until the liquid has been absorbed. Continue until you have used all the liquid, about 20 minutes. Stir in the cheese and season with cracked black pepper and sea salt. Pour onto a large plate and spread out to cool.

To make the suppli, take tablespoons of cooled risotto and form 16 balls. With your forefinger make a dent in each risotto ball and place an olive in the center. Roll the risotto ball in your hand to reshape and cover the olive.

Dust the suppli balls with flour, dip into the beaten egg, and then toss in the breadcrumbs until well coated. At this stage they can be left to rest in the fridge for up to 6 hours until you are ready to cook.

Heat the oil in a heavy-bottomed pan until the oil reaches 180°C (350°F) on a deep-frying thermometer. Alternatively, test the oil by dropping in a cube of bread. It should turn golden brown in about 20 seconds.

Fry the suppli in batches until crispy and golden brown, about 2 minutes. Drain on paper towels. Sprinkle generously with saffron salt and serve.

GAZPACHO WITH SMOKED SALTED CROUTONS

I like to make gazpacho with heirloom tomatoes of different colors, but if you can't find them, use any very ripe and tasty tomatoes. The sherry vinegar is the key to gazpacho, so seek out a heady one from Jerez in Spain—it will make all the difference.

3 lbs./1.3 kg heirloom tomatoes
1 garlic clove
1 small red onion
2 Persian cucumbers
1 green (bell) pepper
1 Serrano chile/chilli (red or green)
1/4 cup/60 ml extra virgin olive oil
1/4 cup/60 ml Jerez sherry vinegar
sel gris and cracked black pepper
olive oil, to drizzle

SMOKED SALTED CROUTONS
1 small baguette
1 garlic clove, finely chopped
1/4 cup/60 ml olive oil
1 tablespoon smoked sea salt

a 6-cup/1.5-litre food processor

SERVES 4

To peel the tomatoes, fill a small bowl with ice and water and set aside. Bring a medium-size pot of water to a boil. Using a sharp knife, score a cross in the top of each tomato. Drop the tomatoes into the hot water for 30 seconds. Remove with a slotted spoon and drop into the iced water for 1 minute. Remove from the water and peel. Cut the tomatoes into halves or quarters, depending on their size, and put in the food processor.

Roughly chop the garlic, onion, and cucumbers and add to the tomatoes. Cut the green (bell) pepper and Serrano chile/chilli in half and remove the white pith and seeds. Chop and add to the tomatoes. Pulse the tomato mixture until it is chunky. Pour the gazpacho into a large bowl and stir in the olive oil and Jerez sherry vinegar. Season with sel gris and cracked black pepper then chill in the fridge until ready to serve.

Preheat the oven to 200°C (400°F) Gas 6.

To make the smoked salted croutons, slice the baguette lengthwise into quarters and lay the slices on a baking sheet. Mix the garlic and olive oil in a small bowl and drizzle over the bread. Sprinkle with the smoked sea salt and bake in the preheated oven for 8–10 minutes until golden.

Pour the gazpacho into serving bowls and drizzle with olive oil. Serve with the croutons on the side.

WATERMELON & RICOTTA SALATA SALAD
WITH OLIVE SALT

This is a delightfully pretty and refreshing salad in which the olive salt brings out the sweetness of the watermelon. Ricotta salata, a lightly salted cheese made from sheep milk, originates from the island of Sicily. If you can't find a mini watermelon, buy the smallest available and cut it in half. You can use Greek feta cheese if ricotta salata isn't available where you are.

1 mini seedless watermelon
6 oz./170 g ricotta salata cheese
2 tablespoons fresh oregano leaves
olive oil, to drizzle
cracked black pepper, to season

OLIVE SALT
10 black olives, pitted/stoned
2½ tablespoons sea salt

SERVES 2

Peel the watermelon and cut it into bite-size chunks. Put in a serving bowl, crumble the ricotta salata over the watermelon, and sprinkle with the oregano.

To make the olive salt, chop the olives roughly. Grind them with the salt using a mortar and pestle until the olives are mashed.

Drizzle the olive oil over the salad and season with black pepper. Sprinkle with a generous amount of the olive salt. Put the remainder of the salt in a bowl to use on other dishes.

PEACH CAPRESE WITH CURRY SALT

Summer, when peaches are in season, is the time to make this salad. The sweet and juicy peaches play off the slightly salty mozzarella, and a sprinkle of curry salt spices up the whole dish.

2 x 8-oz./225-g fresh buffalo
  mozzarella balls
2 large yellow peaches
1 small bunch fresh mint
1 small bunch fresh basil

VINAIGRETTE
1/4 cup/60 ml Champagne vinegar
1/2 cup/125 ml extra virgin olive oil
1/2 teaspoon honey

CURRY SALT
2 tablespoons fleur de sel
2 teaspoons Madras curry powder

SERVES 4

Slice the mozzarella balls into 1/4-inch/5-mm thick slices.

Cut the peaches in half and remove the pits/stones. Slice the peach halves into 1/4-inch/generously 5-mm thick slices. Tear the basil leaves and mint leaves from their stems, reserving 4 sprigs of mint for the garnish.

To make the vinaigrette, put all the ingredients in a small bowl and whisk together.

To make the curry salt, mix together the fleur de sel and curry powder in a small bowl.

To assemble the salad, put a slice of mozzarella on each plate, then top with a slice of peach. Add a few basil and mint leaves and continue to layer until you have used up all the slices of mozzarella and peach.

Drizzle the vinaigrette over the salads and finish with a sprinkle of curry salt. Garnish with a sprig of mint and serve.

ROASTED CHERRY TOMATOES & OLIVES WITH FLEUR DE SEL

This is the perfect dish to serve with fish. It's delicious and simple, with the added bonus of the wonderful aroma of rosemary while it's cooking. Use tiny black Niçoise olives—their intense flavor goes very well with the sweetness of the tomatoes.

1 sprig of fresh rosemary
1 lb./450 g cherry tomatoes
1/2 cup/90 g Niçoise olives, pitted/stoned
cracked black pepper and fleur de sel, to taste

SERVES 4

Preheat the oven to 190°C (375°F) Gas 5.

Run your fingers down the rosemary sprig, tearing the leaves off as you go. It will yield about 2 tablespoons of leaves.

In a bowl toss together the rosemary, tomatoes, and olives. Season with cracked black pepper.

Pour the tomato mixture onto a non-stick baking sheet or pan. Roast in the preheated oven for 10 minutes, until the tomatoes have some color and have softened. Remove from the oven and shake the pan. Set aside to cool for a few minutes.

Put the tomatoes in a bowl, sprinkle with the fleur de sel, and serve.

BARBECUE CORN ON THE COB WITH SMOKED PAPRIKA BUTTER

Cook corn cobs on the barbecue, tear off the outer husks, and slather them in smoked paprika butter to enjoy the deep, smoky flavors. Any leftover butter will go well with any grilled meat. You can keep it in the fridge for up to 1 week.

2 sticks/225 g unsalted butter, at room temperature
2 teaspoons sweet smoked paprika
1 teaspoon smoked sea salt
6 corn on the cob, husks still on

SERVES 6

Put the butter in a food processor with the paprika and smoked sea salt. Mix until the butter is smooth. Refrigerate until ready to use.

Preheat a barbecue grill.

Put the corn cobs, with the husks still on, on the hot barbecue grill. Cook for 3 minutes, turn over, and cook for another 3 minutes. You want the corn to have a crunch when you bite into it.

When the corn is ready, remove from the heat and tear back the outer husk. You can use the husk as a handle. Spread the smoked paprika butter over the corn and eat immediately.

FRIED GREEN TOMATOES WITH SUMMER PICKLES

This is a big taste of the South right here. Green tomatoes lightly tossed in a spicy cornmeal, then fried until crisp and golden brown. Served alongside a beautiful pile of summer pickles, there is nothing better. It's a meal in itself. Don't try to substitute ripe tomatoes—it just isn't the same.

6 large green tomatoes
vegetable oil, to cook
coarse sea salt, to serve

SUMMER PICKLES
1 lb./450 g mixed summer
    vegetables, such as zucchini/
    courgette, beans, beets/beetroot,
    and (bell) peppers
2 cups/480 ml red wine vinegar
1/2 cup/100 g granulated/caster
    sugar
1 teaspoon black peppercorns
1 teaspoon yellow mustard seeds
1 1/2 tablespoons sea salt

FRIED GREEN TOMATO SPICE MIX
1 cup/150 g fine-grain cornmeal
2 tablespoons coarse cornmeal/
    polenta
1/2 teaspoon cayenne pepper
1/2 teaspoon dried garlic powder
1/2 teaspoon hot red pepper/dried
    chilli flakes
1 teaspoon dried oregano
1 teaspoon dried basil
1/2 teaspoon ground black pepper
1/4 teaspoon Kosher/table salt

a cast iron pan

SERVES 4–6

To make the pickles, cut the vegetables into bite-size batons and layer in a ceramic baking dish.

Put all the remaining ingredients for the Summer Pickle in a non-reactive saucepan and bring to a boil. Pour the hot liquid over the vegetables, cover, and set aside for 4–24 hours. When ready to eat, remove the vegetables from the pickling liquor and pile up in a serving bowl.

Wash the tomatoes under cold water and slice them into 1/2-inch/1-cm discs. Mix all of the ingredients for the Fried Green Tomato Spice Mix together and tip into a shallow bowl. Lightly toss the tomato slices in it.

Heat a cast iron pan over a medium–high heat and coat with vegetable oil. Put a single layer of tomatoes in the pan and cook for about 3–5 minutes until golden brown. Turn the tomatoes over and continue to cook until crispy and golden brown. Remove the cooked tomatoes to a platter and continue to cook the remainder in batches.

Sprinkle liberally with coarse sea salt and serve immediately with a bowl of the Summer Pickles.

PADRON PEPPERS WITH SEL GRIS

These little Spanish peppers are a favorite tapas dish. Luckily they are also one of the easiest to prepare and good salt is essential to finish the dish. Be warned—although mostly mildly peppery, one in every dozen Padron peppers has a fiery hit, so have a glass of cold beer to hand!

1/4 cup/60 ml olive oil
1 lb./450 g Padron peppers
sel gris, to sprinkle

SERVES 4–6

Put a sauté pan over a high heat. When it starts to smoke, turn the heat down to medium. Add the olive oil and swirl the pan once to cover the base with oil.

Add the Padron peppers and cook until slightly blistered. Sprinkle generously with the sel gris and serve straightaway—they can be eaten fresh from the pan or tipped into a bowl but always with your fingers!

GOATS' CHEESE DIP
WITH CITRUS SALT

I love this dip made with goats' milk yogurt.
It is perfect as a light snack in warm weather,
served with pita chips, cut raw vegetables,
or bread. Alternatively, a large dollop turns
a simple fish cake into something special.

2 lbs./900 g goats' milk yogurt, preferably organic
extra virgin olive oil, to drizzle

CITRUS SALT
finely grated zest of 1 lemon
2 tablespoons rock salt granules

a cheesecloth/muslin square

MAKES 2 CUPS/1 KG

Line a strainer/sieve with cheesecloth/muslin,
a single layer of paper towels or a coffee filter.

Rest the lined strainer/sieve on the rim of
a bowl deep enough to catch the drained fluid.
Empty the goats' milk yogurt into the lined
strainer/sieve, cover with plastic wrap/clingfilm,
and leave in the fridge overnight.

Make the citrus salt by pounding the lemon
zest and salt in a mortar and pestle. Transfer
to a small bowl.

The next day, remove the goats' cheese from
the fridge and discard the liquid. Put the cheese
in a serving bowl. Drizzle with olive oil and
sprinkle with the citrus salt to serve.

SWEET POTATO WEDGES
WITH HAWAIIAN RED ALAEA SEA SALT

As well as being very tasty, this is a pretty dish
to look at. The beautiful orange flesh and dark
red skins of the garnet sweet potatoes are offset
by the ocher-colored salt. Hawaiian red alaea
sea salt is a garnishing salt only, rich in minerals
that give it such a vivid color. When cooked,
it loses both its color and flavor.

2 lbs./900 g garnet sweet potatoes
   (about 3), skin on
1/4 cup/60 ml olive oil
cracked black pepper
Hawaiian red alaea sea salt, to serve

SERVES 4

Preheat the oven to 190°C (375°F) Gas 5.

Rinse and dry the sweet potatoes. Cut them into
thick wedges and arrange on a non-stick baking
sheet. Pour the olive oil over them, tossing the
wedges to make sure they are evenly coated.
Season with cracked black pepper.

Bake in the preheated oven for 10 minutes.
Turn the wedges over and return to the oven for
another 10–15 minutes, until golden brown and
crispy on the edges. Pierce the wedges with
a sharp knife to make sure they are cooked all
the way through.

Remove from the oven, sprinkle generously
with Hawaiian red alaea sea salt, and serve.

SWEET THINGS & DRINKS

SUMMER SHORTCAKE WITH PEPPERED STRAWBERRIES

In summer, when strawberry season arrives, it's the time to make these divine little shortcakes. With lashings of thick mascarpone tucked in between, this is a dessert to remember.

2 cups/280 g sliced strawberries
1 cup/225 g mascarpone

SHORTBREAD
1½ cups/200 g all-purpose/plain flour, plus extra for dusting
2 teaspoons baking powder
3 tablespoons turbinado or demerara sugar, plus extra for sprinkling
4 tablespoons/60 g cold butter, cut into small pieces
½ teaspoon sea salt
⅔ cup plus 2 tablespoons/190 ml heavy/double cream, cold

SYRUP
1 cup/200 g white sugar
1 teaspoon freshly cracked black Malabar peppercorns

a 3-inch/7.5-cm round cookie cutter
a baking sheet lined with baking parchment

SERVES 6

Preheat the oven to 190°C (375°F) Gas 5.

Put the flour, baking powder, turbinado or demerara sugar, butter, and salt in a food processor and pulse until the mixture resembles large breadcrumbs. Pour in the cream and continue to pulse until the mixture just comes together.

Turn the dough out on to a lightly floured worksurface and roll out to a thickness of 1 inch/2.5 cm. Using the cookie cutter, cut out 6 circles. Arrange the shortcakes on the lined baking sheet 1 inch/2.5 cm apart and sprinkle with the extra sugar. Bake in the preheated oven for 20 minutes.

To make the syrup, place the sugar and peppercorns in a small pan with ½ cup/120 ml water over a medium–high heat. Bring to a boil, stirring occasionally, until the sugar has dissolved. Reduce to a simmer and cook for 10 minutes, then remove from the heat and strain into a bowl. Add the sliced strawberries and cool.

To serve, split the shortcakes in half. Generously spread the bottom halves with mascarpone and spoon the strawberries and syrup on top. Place the shortcake tops on and serve.

GOATS' CHEESE PANNA COTTA
WITH CANDIED PEPPERED CHERRIES

Delicate goats' cheese panna cotta topped with sweet, heady candied cherries will make your guests very happy. If you can't find goats' milk yogurt, then just use regular full-fat yogurt. In winter I top it with peppery candied blood oranges.

PANNA COTTA
2 teaspoons gelatin
2 cups/475 ml heavy/double cream
1/2 cup/100 g white sugar
4 oz./115 g soft goats' cheese, at room temperature
1 cup/215 g goats' milk yogurt

CANDIED PEPPERED CHERRIES
1/2 cup/100 g white sugar
1 teaspoon crushed pink peppercorns
2 cups/300 g pitted/stoned cherries, halved

SERVES 6

Dissolve the gelatin in 2 tablespoons of warm water and set aside.

Bring the cream and sugar to a boil in a pan over a medium–high heat, stirring constantly. Reduce the heat to a simmer and continue to cook for 5 minutes, until the sugar has completely dissolved. Remove from the heat and whisk in the goats' cheese, yogurt, and gelatin until smooth.

Pour into six heatproof glasses or ramekins and set aside to cool, then cover and refrigerate for 4–24 hours.

To make the syrup for the cherries, place the sugar and peppercorns in a small pan with 60 ml/1/4 cup water over a medium–high heat. Bring to a boil, stirring occasionally, until the sugar has dissolved, then reduce the heat to a simmer and cook for 10 minutes. Remove from the heat, add the cherries, and set aside to cool.

To serve, spoon the cooled candied peppered cherries and their syrup on top of the panna cotta.

PEPPER BOURBON CHOCOLATE POTS

Delightful little pots packed with spicy, boozy flavors. I like to make these for casual outside dinners in the summer. They are a breeze to whip up and are also great for picnics—I pour the mousse into easily transportable individual jars with lids.

2/3 cup/140 ml heavy/double cream
2 teaspoons good-quality instant espresso powder
2 teaspoons Lampong peppercorns, coarsely chopped
1 tablespoon bourbon or whiskey
10½ oz./300 g dark/bittersweet chocolate (72% cocoa solids)
6 egg whites
2 tablespoons superfine/caster sugar
crème fraîche, to serve
edible flowers, to garnish (optional)

SERVES 6

Pour the cream into a small pan and add the espresso powder and peppercorns. Bring to a boil, stirring constantly, then remove from the heat and cool. Strain through a fine sieve into a small bowl, then stir in the bourbon or whiskey.

Melt the chocolate over a medium heat in a double boiler, or in a heatproof bowl set over a pan of simmering water. Remove from the heat and stir in the espresso pepper cream to combine. Set aside.

In a large bowl whisk the egg whites with an electric beater until stiff peaks form, then add the sugar and whisk to combine.

Add the chocolate mixture to the egg whites a spoonful at a time and gently fold together. Divide the mixture between six small bowls or pots. Refrigerate for 4–24 hours.

To serve, add a dollop of crème fraîche to the top of each chocolate pot. If you wish, garnish with edible flowers.

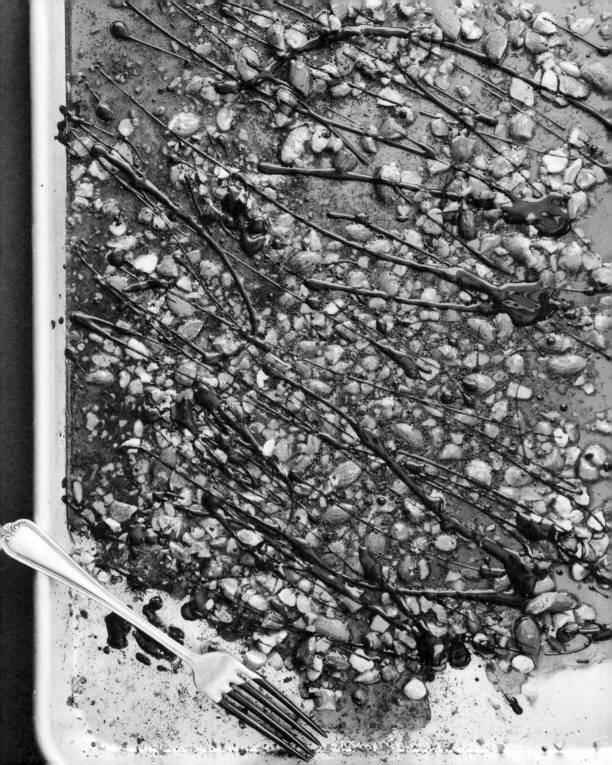

MEXICAN PRALINE

Wonderful spicy chili/chilli powder, pepper, and smoked paprika spike against the almonds and sweetness of the praline. If you wish, you can omit the chocolate swirled on top. Fun to serve at a dinner party as one big dramatic sheet for guests to break, or crush up and serve sprinkled on top of ice cream.

1½ cups/200 g raw almonds, coarsely chopped
2 teaspoons ancho chili/chilli powder
2 teaspoons cracked rainbow peppercorns
½ teaspoon smoked paprika
3 cups/600 g white sugar
3½ oz./100 g bittersweet/dark chocolate (72% cocoa solids)

a large baking sheet, lightly oiled

MAKES ENOUGH TO GARNISH 6 DESSERTS

Put the almonds, chili/chilli powder, peppercorns, and smoked paprika in a saucepan over a medium–high heat and toast for 2–3 minutes. Tip out onto the prepared baking sheet and spread evenly.

Pour the sugar into a medium saucepan, add ⅔ cup/150 ml water, and bring to a boil over medium–high heat. Boil the syrup undisturbed for approximately 8–10 minutes until it is a dark golden brown and the sugar has dissolved. You can swirl the pan as the syrup darkens. Pour evenly over the almond mixture and allow to set.

Melt the chocolate over a medium heat in a double boiler, or in a heatproof bowl set over a pan of simmering water. Using a fork, drizzle the melted chocolate over the praline and allow to set.

Store in an airtight container for up to 1 week.

PFEFFERNUSSE COOKIES

Very popular at Christmas time, these German cookies are filled with spices and pepper. You can dust them lightly with peppered sugar or completely coat them to make them festive. If there should be any left over, they make a lovely addition to a trifle.

2¼ cups/300 g all-purpose/
    plain flour
1 teaspoon ground ginger
½ teaspoon ground cinnamon
½ teaspoon ground allspice
¼ teaspoon ground nutmeg
¼ teaspoon baking soda/
    bicarbonate of soda
2 teaspoons finely ground
    white pepper
1 stick/115 g butter, at room
    temperature
³/₄ cup/150 g soft dark brown sugar
¼ cup/85 g molasses
    or dark treacle
1 egg
½ cup/70 g confectioner's/
    icing sugar

2 baking sheets lined with baking
    parchment

MAKES ABOUT 36

Sift the flour, ginger, cinnamon, allspice, nutmeg, baking soda/bicarbonate of soda, and half the pepper into a bowl.

Put the butter, sugar, and molasses in the bowl of an electric mixer and beat for about 5 minutes until fluffy. Add the egg and continue to beat until fully combined. Reduce the speed and slowly beat in the flour mixture.

Scoop out 1 tablespoon of dough at a time and roll into balls. Place on the prepared baking sheets 2 inches/5 cm apart. Put in the freezer for 15 minutes.

Preheat the oven to 175°C (350°F) Gas 4.

Remove the cookies from the freezer and bake in the preheated oven for 15 minutes until golden brown. Transfer to wire racks to cool.

In a small bowl, mix together the confectioner's/icing sugar and remaining pepper. When the cookies have completely cooled, sprinkle with the sugar mix.

Store in an airtight container for up to 2 weeks.

CHOCOLATE SEA SALT COOKIES

You may think this combination sounds a little odd, but trust me this is a divine cookie. One bite and you will feel the explosion of tastes between the dark rich sweetness of the chocolate and fleur de sel salt. Use only the best fleur de sel from Guérande in France.

1 cup/140 g all-purpose/plain flour
1/2 cup/40 g unsweetened cocoa powder
1/2 teaspoon baking powder
1/2 teaspoon baking soda/ bicarbonate of soda
12 oz./120 g bittersweet/dark chocolate (70% cocoa solids), roughly chopped
1 stick plus 3 tablespoons/ 170 g unsalted butter, at room temperature
3/4 cup/85 g dark brown sugar
1/4 cup/40 g superfine/caster sugar
1 egg
1 teaspoon pure vanilla extract
1 teaspoon rum
fleur de sel, to sprinkle

2 baking sheets, lined with baking parchment

MAKES APPROXIMATELY 24

Preheat the oven to 180°C (350°F) Gas 4.

Sift together the flour, cocoa powder, baking powder, and baking soda/bicarbonate of soda and set aside.

Melt 4 oz./40 g bittersweet/dark chocolate, either in a bowl over a saucepan of simmering water or in a microwave.

Cream together the butter and sugars in the bowl of an electric stand mixer or using an electric handheld beater on high speed until light and fluffy, scraping down the sides of the bowl if necessary. Add the egg, vanilla extract, rum, and melted chocolate. Continue to beat for 2 minutes. Reduce the speed to slow and add the flour mixture. When that is well mixed, stir in the remaining chopped chocolate.

Put the mixture in the fridge for 5 minutes just to harden slightly.

Scoop tablespoons of the mixture onto the lined baking sheets, 2 inches/5 cm apart. Flatten slightly with the back of the scoop. Sprinkle a little fleur de sel on top of each cookie and bake in the preheated oven for 10 minutes. Store in an airtight container for up to 1 week.

MEXICAN CHILI CHOCOLATE SALTED TRUFFLES

A spicy taste from south of the border, these salty chili/chilli chocolate truffles, rolled in Mexican Ibarra chocolate and Himalayan pink rock salt, are divine! You won't be able to stop eating them. Mexican Ibarra chocolate disks are made with chocolate mixed with cocoa beans and cinnamon. Buy them at Latin food markets or online.

8 oz./220 g bittersweet/dark chocolate (70% cocoa solids), roughly chopped
1/4 cup/60 ml pouring cream
1 tablespoon/15 g unsalted butter
1/2 teaspoon confectioner's chili/chilli oil

SALTED COCOA DUSTING POWDER
3 oz./90 g Ibarra chocolate disks, roughly chopped
1 tablespoon Himalayan pink rock salt

a melon baller

MAKES 40

Put the chopped chocolate, cream, and butter in a heatproof bowl. Place over a pan of simmering water, making sure the water does not touch the bottom of the bowl. Once the chocolate has started to melt, stir gently until the mixture is smooth and creamy.

Stir in the chili/chilli oil and pour the mixture into a shallow bowl. Refrigerate until firm.

To make the dusting powder, process the Ibarra chocolate to a powder in a food processor. Pour it into a bowl and mix in the Himalayan salt.

When the chocolate mixture has set, scoop out the truffles with the melon baller and roll into balls. Toss in the dusting powder and serve.

Cook's Note You can adjust the amount of chili/chilli oil to taste. If you can't find Ibarra chocolate, you can make a similar dusting powder by mixing the following ingredients together: 1/3 cup/55 g white sugar, 1/3 cup/20 g cocoa powder, 1 teaspoon ground cinnamon, and 1 tablespoon Himalayan pink rock salt.

CHAI TEA

Chai tea is one of those wonderful drinks that everyone has their own recipe for and there can be long, dizzying conversations debating it, especially while sipping it. Drink it hot or cold, and add a few little extras to make it your own.

1 teaspoon ground ginger
4–6 cardamom pods, bruised
1 cinnamon stick
2 star anise
1 teaspoon Tellicherry peppercorns
1/2 teaspoon whole cloves
2 teaspoons black tea
milk, to taste

SERVES 1

Put all the ingredients apart from the tea and milk in a pan along with 1 cup/250 ml water. Bring to a boil and cook for 2 minutes. Remove from the heat, add the tea, and allow to steep for 5 minutes.

Strain into a cup or glass and add milk as desired. Add ice for a chilled version.

CHAI APPLES (pictured p.22)

Layer 4 apples, cored and thinly sliced, with 1 cup/150 g of dried cranberries and 1 tablespoon of green peppercorns in a sterilized jar. Bring the Basic Pickle Mix (p. 23) to a boil, adding 1 teaspoon of ground mixed chai spices used above (or a packet mix) and stirring to dissolve the sugar. Cook for 3 minutes, then pour into a sterilized jar and screw the lid on. Seal following the instructions on p.23.

MANGO PEPPER BOBA

Boba (bubble tea) is a sweet Taiwanese drink made with large tapioca pearls. It comes in a kaleidoscope of colors and flavors. This is to be sipped slowly on a hot day, without getting the pearls stuck in your straw! Wide straws are best.

1/4 cup/60 ml Simple Syrup (p.136)
6 kaffir lime leaves
2 cups/340 g chopped mango, fresh or frozen
2 cups/350 g ice chips/crushed ice
1 teaspoon Lampong peppercorns
1 cup/75 g cooked boba pearls (large tapioca balls)

SERVES 4

Heat the syrup in a small pan, add the lime leaves, then remove from the heat and set aside to cool.

Place the cooled lime leaf-infused syrup, mango, ice chips/crushed ice, and peppercorns in a blender and process until smooth. Divide the pearls between the glasses, then top with the mango juice.

Add a wide straw to each drink and serve.

PEPPER & LEMON-INFUSED VODKA

This is a great way to infuse vodka. You can ring the changes and use other peppercorns, citrus, and chiles/chillies. I like to use a Meyer lemon, as they have a wonderful perfume and aroma. Store in the freezer for an icy evening cocktail.

1 Meyer lemon
24–34 fl oz./70 cl–1 litre/bottle of good-quality vodka
2 strings of brined green peppercorns

MAKES 1 BOTTLE

Cut the lemon into thin slices. Start layering by dropping a few pieces of lemon into the vodka bottle (or use a sterilized, wide-necked bottle) and add a string of peppercorns. Repeat, ending with a layer of lemon.

Seal and shake the bottle, then store in a dark cool place for 1 month. Thereafter, store in the freezer until ready to use so it is kept ice cold.

PEPPERED LEMON DROP

When the sun is low in the sky and it's cocktail hour, the Lemon Drop is always welcome. Understated in its simplicity, it has a kick from the tart lemons and spicy infused peppercorn vodka. Sit back and sip slowly.

2 teaspoons crushed green peppercorns
1 teaspoon sugar
crushed ice
2 fl. oz./55 ml Pepper & Lemon-infused Vodka (left)
2 tablespoons/30 ml freshly squeezed lemon juice
2 tablespoons simple syrup (see recipe below and method)

SIMPLE SYRUP
1 cup/225 g fine white sugar
1 cup/150 ml cold water

SERVES 1

First make the simple syrup. Put the sugar and water in a small pan over a medium heat. Simmer until all of the sugar has dissolved, then set aside to cool completely.

Mix together the crushed peppercorns and sugar on a small plate. Wet the rim of the glass and dip it into the pepper sugar and set aside.

Fill a cocktail shaker with crushed ice and pour in the vodka, lemon juice, and simple syrup. Shake vigorously and pour into the pepper-rimmed glass.

FROZEN PEACH MARGARITA
WITH MURRAY RIVER SALT

My peach Margarita is best made in season when peaches are ripe and juicy, but you can also use frozen peaches. The chipotle salt adds a taste of Mexico. Salud!

$1/4$ teaspoon chipotle powder
1 tablespoon Murray River salt flakes
$1/4$ cup/60 ml tequila
1 oz./30 ml peach schnapps
1 large fresh peach, pitted/stoned and quartered,
    or 8 oz./225 g frozen peaches
2 cups/450 g crushed ice
finely grated zest and freshly squeezed juice of 1 lime
    (halves reserved)

SERVES 1

Mix together the chipotle powder and Murray River salt flakes. Wet the rim of a glass with the squeezed lime and dip into the chipotle salt. Set aside.

Put the remaining ingredients in a blender and blend until smooth. Serve in the salted glass.

MANNY'S MOJITO WITH SEA SALT

This mojito recipe is from my friend Manuel Rodriguez. He simply serves his citrus cocktail in pitchers, but I like to dust the rim of each glass with a pretty coating of lime salt.

finely grated zest of 1 lime
4 tablespoons sea salt flakes
1 large bunch fresh mint, plus extra for garnishing
2 cups/500 ml white rum
1 cup/250 ml simple syrup (p.136)
3 cups/750 ml freshly squeezed lime juice,
    about 12 limes (halves reserved)
2 cups/500 ml club soda/soda water
crushed ice, to fill

SERVES 6

Mix the lime zest and sea salt, spread out on a small plate, and set aside.

Muddle the mint and rum in a large pitcher/ jug by mashing the mint against the side of the pitcher with the back of a wooden spoon. Leave for 30 minutes to let the flavors mingle.

Add the simple syrup, lime juice, and club soda/ soda water to the rum and stir. Add enough crushed ice to fill the pitcher/jug. Garnish with mint sprigs.

Wet the rim of a tall glass with a squeezed lime, then dip the glass in the salt mixture and turn once. Do the same with the rest of the glasses then fill up with Manny's Mojito.

MARTINI
WITH SALTED BLACK OLIVES

Dry-cured black olives make for a very hip martini. These Moroccan olives are picked ripe from the tree, washed and dried in the sun, then salted and packed in jars. Skewer them on a rosemary sprig for extra flavor and wow factor.

3 cured black olives, pitted/stoned
1 sprig of fresh rosemary 1 teaspoon dry vermouth,
    such as Noilly Prat
¼ cup/60 ml gin
ice cubes, to fill

a cocktail shaker

SERVES 1

Skewer the olives on the rosemary sprig. Pour the vermouth into a chilled glass, swirl, and pour out.

Fill a cocktail shaker with ice and pour in the gin. Shake and strain the gin into the glass.

Garnish with the olive skewer and serve immediately.

BLOODY MARY
WITH CELERY SALT

This classic brunch drink, just gets better with a rim of celery salt. When making the celery salt, the leaves are dried in the oven on a wire rack so that warm air can circulate around the leaves.

1 small bunch celery, with leaves
1 tablespoon Jurassic salt
5 cups/1.25 litres tomato juice, chilled
1 cup/250 ml citron vodka, chilled
1 tablespoon Worcestershire sauce
2 teaspoons hot sauce or Tabasco sauce
1 tablespoon balsamic vinegar
grated zest and freshly squeezed juice of 1 lemon
    (halves reserved)
cracked green peppercorns
ice cubes, to fill

SERVES 4

Preheat the oven to its lowest setting. Pick the leaves from the celery, place them on a wire rack, and put in the oven for 10–15 minutes until they are dried. Remove and let cool.

Put the dried celery leaves and Jurassic salt in a mini food processor or a salt grinder, grind, and empty onto a small plate. Wet the rims of 4 glasses with the reserved lemon halves and dip them in the celery salt.

Fill a pitcher/jug with ice and pour in the tomato juice, vodka, Worcestershire sauce, hot sauce, balsamic vinegar, and lemon zest and juice. Season liberally with peppercorns and a little of the celery salt. Stir and pour into the salted glasses. Garnish with a celery stick and serve.

INDEX

PICTURE CREDITS

Photography on the following pages by:

Steve Baxter page 1

Jonathan Gregson pages 2 bl and ar,
5–11, 18l, 26–29, 30 bl and r, 38–45,
46al, 58–67, 68 al and br, 83–88, 95,
96 ar and bl, 103–111, 115, 116, 118r,
130–133, 138–141, front endpapers

Erin Kunkel 2 al and br, 4, 13–17, 18r,
21–25, 30al, 33–37, 46 bl and r, 49–57,
68 ar and bl, 71–80, 91, 92, 96 al and
br, 99, 100, 112, 118l, 121–129,
134–137, 144 back endpapers